SECURITY, GOVERNANCE, AND DEMOCRATIC RIGHTS

ESSAYS ON THE NORTH-EAST

SECURITY, GOVERNANCE, AND DEMOCRATIC RIGHTS

ESSAYS ON THE NORTH-EAST

Edited by

K.S. SUBRAMANIAN

NIYOGI BOOKS

Published by

NIYOGI BOOKS

D-78, Okhla Industrial Area, Phase-I
New Delhi-110 020, INDIA
Tel: 91-11-26816301, 49327000
Fax: 91-11-26810483, 26813830
email: niyogibooks@gmail.com
website: www.niyogibooksindia.com

Editor: P.K. Jayanthan
Design: Shashi Bhushan Prasad

Cover image courtesy: Wikimedia Commons, available in the public domain

ISBN: 978-93-83098-13-2
Publication: 2014

Printed at: Niyogi Offset Pvt. Ltd., New Delhi, India

Contents

List of Abbreviations

AASU	All Assam (Asom) Students' Union
ACT	affected citizens of Teesta
ADB	Asian Development Bank
AFSPA	Armed Forces (Special Powers) Act, 1958
AGP	Asom Gana Parishad
AGSP	Asom Gana Sangram Parishad
AJM	Assam Jatiya Mahasabha
AJYCP	Assam Jatiyatabadi Yuba Chhatra Parishad
AMKIL	Apunba Manipur Kanba Imma Lup
AMSU	All Manipur Students' Union
AMUCO	All Manipur United Clubs Organization
ANVC	Achik National Volunteer Council
AR	Assam Rifles
BIMSTEC	Bay of Bengal Initiative for Multi-Sectoral Technical and Economic Cooperation
CAG	Comptroller and Auditor General
CAPFs	Central Armed Police Forces
CBI	Central Bureau of Investigation
CCC	Concerned Citizens' Committee
CEA	Central Electricity Authority

CM	chief minister
CNF	Chin National Front
CPB	Communist Party of Burma
CPFs	Central Paramilitary Forces
CPI(M)	Communist Party of India (Maoist)
CrPC	criminal procedure code
CRPF	Central Reserve Police Force
DAA	Disturbed Areas Act
DAN	Democratic Alliance of Nagaland
DC	Deputy Commissioner
DDR	disarmament, demobilisation and reintegration
DGFI	Directorate General of Forces Intelligence
DHD	Dima Halam Deogah
DIG	Deputy Inspector General
DM	District Magistrate
DONER	Development of the North Eastern Region
DPRs	detailed project reports
DRDA	District Rural Development Agency
DSG	Delhi Solidarity Group
EAC	Expert Appraisal Committee
EIA	Environmental Impact Assessment
EIC	East India Company
FNR	Forum for Naga Reconciliation
GoI	Government of India
HQ	headquarters
IB	Intelligence Bureau
ICDS	Integrated Child Development Services
ICS	Indian Civil Service
ICSSR	Indian Council of Social Science Research
IDP	internally displaced person
IMG	inter-ministerial group
IPC	Indian Penal Code
IRB	India Reserve Battalion

IRP	integrated resource planning
ISI	Inter-Services Intelligence
J&K	Jammu and Kashmir
JAF	joint action forum
JCE	joint court of enquiry
JE	junior engineer
KIA	Kachin Independence Army
KLA	Kuki Liberation Army
KLNF	Kuki Longri National Front
KLO	Kamtapur Liberation Organization
KSA	Kangleipak Students' Association
LEP	Look East Policy
MEA	Ministry of External Affairs
MHA	Ministry of Home Affairs
MHRC	Manipur Human Rights Commission
MoA	memorandum of agreement
MoEF	Ministry of Environment and Forests
MoU	memorandum of understanding
MPs	members of Parliament
MR	Manipur Rifles
MSF	Manipur Students' Federation
NBWL	National Board for Wildlife
NCHAC	North Cachar Hills Autonomous Council
NCPCR	National Commission for Protection of Child Rights
NDFB	National Democratic Front of Bodoland
NEAA	National Environmental Appellate Authority
NEC	North Eastern Council
NEFA	North Eastern Frontier Agency
NEHU	North-Eastern Hill University
NGO	non-governmental organisation
NHRC	National Human Rights Commission
NIH	National Institutes of Health, US
NMA	Naga Mothers' Association

NNC	Naga National Council
NPC	National Police Commission
NPMHR	Naga Peoples' Movement for Human Rights
NREGS	National Rural Employment Guarantee Scheme
NRHM	National Rural Health Mission
NSA	National Security Act
NSCN	National Socialist Council of Nagaland
NSCN(IM)	National Socialist Council of Nagaland (Isak Muivah)
NSF	Naga Students' Federation
OBCs	other backward classes
PAs	protected areas
PCG	People's Consultative Group
PD	project director
PDS	public distribution system
PF	provident fund
PHE	public health engineering
PLA	People's Liberation Army
PM	prime minister
PMO	prime minister's office
POTA	Prevention of Terrorism Act
PTSD	post-traumatic stress disorder
R&P	Research and Policy
RTI	right to information
SBI	State Bank of India
SC	Supreme Court
SGRY	Swarnajayanti Gramin Rozgar Yojana
SIA	social impact assessment
SIPHRO	Sinlung Indigenous People's Human Rights Organisation
SJA	Sanmilita Jatiya Abhibartan (United National Conference)
SP	Superintendent of Police
SSA	Sarva Shiksha Abhiyan
SSP	Senior Superintendent of Police
TIS	Transparency International Surveys

ToR	terms of reference
UAPA	Unlawful Activities (Prevention) Act, 2004
UDHR	Universal Declaration of Human Rights
UKLF	United Kuki Liberation Front
ULFA	United Liberation Front of Asom
UNC	United Naga Council
UNHCHR	UN High Commissioner for Human Rights
UNLF	United National Liberation Front
UPDS	United People's Democratic Solidarity
UWSA	United Wa State Army
VCDC	Village Council Development Committee
WB	World Bank
ZSI	Zoological Survey of India

Preface

The essays collected in this volume are the outcome of a seminar held in 2011 at the Indian Council of Social Science Research (ICSSR) Regional Centre, Shillong. Though belated, we are happy to bring out this book.

As a Senior Fellow at ICSSR during 2011–12, I undertook a study of the important issue of violation of democratic rights in the North-East, especially in Manipur, in the name of suppression of militant activities. Earlier in November 2009, I was part of a fact-finding mission which travelled to the state to investigate and report on the extrajudicial killing of two innocent youngsters, Sanjit and Ms Rabina by the Manipur police commandos in a crowded market place in the capital city of Imphal.

The Indian Constitution asks the state to undertake measures to reduce inequality and to deliver social justice. The police must play a crucial role in meeting these objectives of the government by maintaining peace and order through just methods. Unfortunately, in Manipur and elsewhere in the region, this task is not being discharged for various reasons. Across the country, the police have not only failed to play this role in most cases but have often been inflicting violence on the people, especially women and children in the North-East causing immense hardship to the people. During the colonial and post-colonial era, the main objectives of the police have been to manage 'public order' and security of state, rather than detection and investigation of crime. Historical and contemporary factors account for this including some provisions of the IPC, CrPC, and the Police Act, 1861. Police in India today have become a 'dangerous anachronism' as noted by a Human Rights Watch report. (Broken System: Dysfunction, Abuse and Impunity in the Indian Police, 2009, New York).

In the context of the North-East in particular, the police and armed forces have been guilty of frequent extrajudicial killings taking advantage of the provisions of extraordinary laws such as the Armed Forces (Special Powers) Act, 1958. This has become particularly notorious in Manipur, a tiny north-eastern state with less than 3 million people.

On taking up my ICSSR project, I felt the need to organise a seminar, involving local scholars and experts to understand and contextualise the specific issues that arose in my mind. This volume is one of the outcomes. The other is a book being published separately titled *State Vs. People: Security Forces, Special Laws and India's North-East*.

I took the help of Dr C.J. Thomas, Deputy Director, North Eastern Regional Centre of ICSSR, Shillong, in identifying participants and organising the seminar. Scholars presented papers on the broad theme of development, conflict, and democratic governance in the region. Representatives of local thinkers, scholars, journalists, activists, bureaucrats, and police personnel were invited to provide insights. The discussions proved fruitful and illuminating and helped carry forward and clarify the thinking on the subjects discussed.

The papers in this volume are arranged under the three heads of Security, Governance, and Democratic Rights. Our concern was to take up issues and themes less focused upon in a most crowded area of studies. Thematically, after reflecting on the policy process, our eminent authors here examine, under **Security**, the themes of environmental security, the peace process in Assam, corruption and insurgency, the Armed Forces (Special Powers) Act, 1958, policing, and small arms proliferation. Under **Governance**, human insecurity in Manipur, grass roots corruption in Assam, and consensual governance in Manipur are discussed. Under **Democratic Rights** issues of conflict and gender and conflict and democratic rights in Nagaland are examined.

The vastness and complexity of the region and the variety and intricacy of its problems have led us to believe that any hasty conclusions about the region as a whole on the basis of the data examined here would be inappropriate. We believe that intensive case studies of problems in each state of the region are the need of the hour. However, our work on the environment reported in the paper on hydroelectric projects deals with their impact on the region as a whole. The recent environmental disaster in Uttarakhand in North India has served to underline the need for a proper study of environmental security in the context of hydroelectric projects in the North-East.

I take this opportunity to thank all those who participated in the seminar and contributed papers. I regret, however, that not all papers presented could be included in this volume due to space constraints. I thank Dr C.J. Thomas and his colleagues for helping me in organising the seminar successfully. I am thankful to Mr Bikash Niyogi, Publisher and Managing Director, his colleagues, and Mr P.K. Jayanthan, editor in bringing out this volume in an admirable manner.

K.S. Subramanian

Reflections on the Policy Process

K.S. Subramanian

When I began to look into the post-independence conflict resolution scenario in north-east India some time ago, I noticed information gaps in two areas of academic studies on the subject: (1) little or no understanding and analysis of Government of India's policy structure and process with regard to conflict resolution in general and that in the North-East in particular (notwithstanding talks of 'counter-insurgency constitutionalism') and (2) lack of policy-relevant case studies of experience in individual states of the region. However, I must note that an official report makes good the former deficiency to some extent (GOI 2008a).

When the British left India in 1947 after transferring power to Indian politicians, they left behind no major institutional arrangement for policy making on conflict situations except the Intelligence Bureau (IB). Set up in 1920, IB provided some basic information though without much analysis, to what later became the Union Ministry of Home Affairs (MHA). B.N. Mullik, as the Director of IB, moved very close to Prime Minister Jawaharlal Nehru and began to play a key role in policy making (Mullik 1972) with regard to issues such as the arrest and detention of Sheikh Abdullah in Jammu and Kashmir (1953), the induction of the army into the Naga Hills of Assam (1955), the forward policy on China (1959), the dismissal of the communist ministry and imposition of President's rule in Kerala (1959) and so on (Subramanian 2007). The Prime Minister, understandably busy with many matters including foreign policy, had perhaps little time to spare and relied heavily on Mullik in formulating his response to internal security emergencies.

It was in 1967, when the Naxalite movement emerged, that the Research and Policy (R&P) Division came up in MHA to explore informed policy options with respect to conflict situations in different parts of the country. The Division produced a well-known report on the Naxalite movement placing it firmly in the context of agrarian tensions, its causes, and trends. It warned that the Green Revolution could turn into a red revolution if appropriate agrarian policy reforms are not undertaken. The report was discussed in Parliament. The then Prime Minister Indira Gandhi urged state governments to institute land reform measures. However, the existence of two different institutions, IB and R&P Division of the MHA, reporting to government on such sensitive matters and often disagreeing with each other (IB, being primarily a police agency, was concerned more with security issues), a conflict situation arose within the ministry leading to the gradual winding up of R&P Division! The lack of institutionalisation of policy mechanisms within the ministry had paralysed the division and that led to MHA's total dependence on the reports provided by IB in understanding and trying to resolve basic conflict issues. The situation came to such a pass that MHA in 2006 found it necessary to rely on IB's understanding of the major conflict situation involving the Maoists as India's biggest 'internal security threat' ignoring other analyses such as the Planning Commission's Expert Group report, which provided a significant study of developmental responses to the Maoist challenges (GOI 2008b).

In studying the government response to violence in the North-East today, one must go back to 1955 and examine the government's decision to induct the army into the Naga Hills area of the undivided

Assam. The decision was arrived at because of the agitation by a section of the people for the independence of Nagas from India. After several years of service in IB and MHA I am clear about the inadequacy of this response. I have discussed this elsewhere (Subramanian 2007 and 2010).

The policy scenario in the Government of India has largely been messy as regards the emerging conflicts in different parts of the country are concerned, particularly in the north-east. The existing institutional mechanisms at the Centre call for drastic reform. The police machinery, a crucial part of the policy structure today, has been described as a 'dangerous anachronism' (HRW 2009). The amaturism and adhocism of policy professionals and the absence of inter-disciplinary inputs of knowledge, skills, vision, and expertise at the top have further vitiated the policy processes.

Disaggregated and policy-relevant case studies on conflict development in each state of the North-East is a prime necessity to avoid the tendency to lump all states together and to suggest policy measures for all of them, which can be deleterious (Choudhury 1999).

MHA is responsible for dealing with conflict situations in the North-East. The Ministry for the Development of the North Eastern Region (DONER) set up in 2004 and the earlier mechanism of the North Eastern Council (NEC) are concerned with development issues. MHA's reliance on past precedents, lack of transparency, its complex relations with IB, and so on are to be explicated. Further, the continued reliance on the controversial Armed Forces (Special Powers) Act, 1958 (AFSPA) and the use of CAPFs for conflict management in the region, ignoring the legitimate role of the state police force, also complicates matters considerably.

The controversial MHA decision in 1955, in spite of opposition from the then Governor of Assam, the army, and the Ministry of External Affairs (MEA), to induct the army into Nagaland, led to the emergence of the Naga rebellion, described as the 'mother of all insurgencies' in the region. The Nagas were not demanding anything other than what the Indian freedom fighters had successfully demanded and achieved from the British (Rustomji 1983).

A former home secretary has noted the deficiencies in policy making at the Government of India level:

> The available expertise at the bureaucratic level to understand, anticipate and evaluate an intricate problem was inadequate and amateurish. The situation in some cases was salvaged in the past because of the flexibility of the system, the sagacity of the political leadership and its openness to information from all quarters (Srinivasavaradan 1992).

The political response to Naxalite/Maoist violence had been based on the perception of socio-economic conditions. After the intensity of the violence had abated, however, recourse had been taken to the standard recipe of deployment of central paramilitary forces ignoring allegations of fake encounters, illegal arrests, and other similar misdeeds.

> In dealing with problems of societal transition, excessive preoccupation with peace and order, ignoring issues of law and justice, can prove expensive in the long run. Lack of steadfastness of purpose is not desirable in dealing with basic nation-building tasks (Srinivasavaradan 1992).

The ad-hocism and amateurism in the field could be remedied only by 'additional inputs of knowledge, skill, and vision and multidisciplinary research and policy analysis' at the top.

The North-East is cradled by five other Asian countries—China, Nepal, Bhutan, Myanmar, and Bangladesh. The states of Arunachal Pradesh, Manipur, Mizoram, and Nagaland share a 1643 km long border with Myanmar. The states of Assam, Meghalaya, Tripura, and Mizoram share a 1880 km long border with Bangladesh. Arunachal

Pradesh, Assam, and Sikkim share a 468 km border with Bhutan. Arunachal Pradesh and Sikkim share a 1325 km border with the Tibetan Autonomous Region of China. The region's difficulties and socio-economic backwardness arising from the loss of connectivity with the rest of India after Partition are well known (Mukherjee 2007). The Look East Policy (LEP) of the Government of India, which combines foreign policy, trade, defence, security, and strategic dimensions, came into existence in 1991. It was, however, only in 2008 that north-east India appeared in a related policy document in the shape of an NER Vision 2020 (GOI 2008c). The voluminous Vision document produced by the Ministry of DONER and NEC fails to provide an Index. Further, among the six authors and six research associates who produced the document, only one was from the North-East (Chakraborty 2012: 33). When the document was released in New Delhi, people in the North-East were indifferent (Chakraborty 2012: 33).

The first two volumes of the document contain general and sectoral strategies, respectively, for the development of the North-East. The third volume contains annexures. Of interest is Chapter 14 in the second volume on 'Governance and Security' (pp. 289–94). Based on the market-oriented development paradigm, the chapter prioritises 'proper law and order' so that any transaction can be carried out in the market without fear of coercion.

The North-East as a whole, minus Sikkim, has been convulsed by conflicts between the State and armed groups and popular movements fighting for a range of demands such as outright secession to greater autonomy within the Indian Constitution. Active negotiations are on to settle the Naga insurgency issue while ceasefire exists with regard to conflicts in Meghalaya, Assam, Manipur, and Tripura. A peace accord was signed in Mizoram in 1986. No less than 40 insurgent groups are said to function in the seven states but only a clutch of them are capable of causing substantial violence. About 15 groups have been banned by the Centre. Though large parts of the region are now free of insurgency, the confrontations have been caused by poor governance, high levels of corruption and political instability. Many of the groups are extortionists and run money making rackets and illegal enterprises. The population and area statistics of the north-eastern states are provided in Annexure I. Annexure II provides data on policemen per every 100 sq. km in the region. Significantly, Assam, Manipur, Tripura, and Nagaland have higher number of policemen per unit of population than the national average.

A significant feature of Vision 2020 is its complete omission, ignoring the public feeling in the North-East, of any discussion on the impact of the controversial AFSPA (Annexure III) on the lives of ordinary people, especially women and children. The serious impact of this extraordinary law on human rights has, however, received attention elsewhere (McDuie-Ra 2009, Kikon 2009, Fernandes 2004, Gaikwad 2009, Navlakha 2011, Barbora 2006).

Another important issue neglected in the Vision 2020 document is the role of Assam Rifles (AR), a central paramilitary force, whose functioning is linked to AFSPA. AR is a special police force created by the British in 1835 to provide security to British establishments in Assam. Subsequent to the creation of several new states in the region in 1972 and the consequent raising of new police forces by them, besides the deployment of other central armed police forces such as the Central Reserve Police Force (CRPF) and the India Reserve Battalions (IRB), however, AR has become an historical anomaly. The counter-insurgency role that AR has been performing controversially so far is best left to state police forces. It should be absolved of its responsibility in the sphere of counter-insurgency. It should be designated to guarding the Indo–Myanmar border. Taking advantage of the immunity from prosecution provided by AFSPA, AR has been guilty of many serious human rights violations in the region. Annexure II provides figures of the police forces available with states in the region between 1978 and 2011. Since law and order is a state subject under the Constitution, it would be proper if these forces are trained adequately to discharge counter-insurgency duties now performed by AR. If this step is taken the controversial AFSPA would become irrelevant much to the relief of the local population. It will also help bring an end to the 12-year long historic fast against AFSPA undertaken by the indomitable Irom Sharmila Chanu of Manipur. The Vision document lists out the following steps taken to ensure peace, security, and human rights in the region:

i. ceasefire agreement with the Isak Muivah Group of National Socialist Council of Nagaland (NSCN) from 1 August 1998;
ii. ceasefire agreement with NSCN (K) group on 28 April 2004;
iii. suspension of operations against the National Democratic Front of Bodoland (NDFB) from 1 June 2005; and
iv. agreement with Dima Halam Deogah (DHD) on 1 January 2003 and with Achik National Volunteer Council (ANVC) on 23 July 2004.
v. Further, the number of IRBs in the region has been raised to 51. This is in addition to state civil armed police (including district armed police) and Central Paramilitary Forces (CPFs) inducted in each state on an ad-hoc basis.

We need to examine the Vision document in terms of its implications for the region not only in terms of trade and commerce but beyond them (Phanjoubam 2007, Chakraborty 2012). It emphasises six development components, that is, (a) self-governance and participatory development, (b) creation of development opportunities, (c) developing sectors with comparative advantage, (d) capacity building of people and institutions, (e) creation of hospitable climate for investment, and (f) infrastructure building through public investment. The 600 page document stresses the need for increasing connectivity and creating employment opportunities through State investment and encouraging private investment in natural resource harnessing, agriculture, and tourism.

LEP aims to enhance India's political and economic relations with countries of the south-east Asian region. It is entwined with India's foreign policy aspirations, strategic initiatives, economic cooperation, and security considerations. However, civil society in the North-East is divided between the State agenda of 'counter-insurgency from above' and 'ethno-nationalist politics of identity from below'.

First, there has been no recorded dissent on the Vision document of which, as already mentioned, only one of the main authors was from the region, namely, Assam.

Second, the benefits accruing from the primary, secondary, and tertiary sectors are not as significant as may be supposed. The rates of unemployment in all states are very high, raising questions on the type of education as well as the kind of development pursued in the region.

Third, border trade is mostly of an informal kind. More vibrant informal trade would be beneficial for all but high transportation costs arising from illegal payments to underground groups, police stations, and forest check posts, apart from legitimate hire charges, make things difficult. Trade openness depends on trade facilitation and transport liberalisation, which is hindered for example, by Indian reservations on the opening of the Stillwell Road between the North-East and Myanmar. The same problem arises with respect to trade liberalisation with Bangladesh.

Fourth, the development agenda spelt out for the North-East involves transfer of resources from the Centre to the state on account of local resource-raising problems. The patron–client relationship between the states and the Centre leads to corruption and lack of accountability. This means further alienation of an already alienated region. Moreover, the spatial entity in the North-East does not coincide with the economic reality with wide variations among and within states. Since each state in the region is small in size, with serious geographical limitations and small markets, it is imperative to develop a common regional market as well as a common development programme for the entire region. Just pumping central funds and stamping of authority through big development projects in the region will lead to dysfunctional development.

Big development in the North-East is always associated with resource extraction by an external authority, usually the State. This leads to dissent and suspicion among the people. The effort to harness the hydroelectric potential of the region by building big dams has led to conflicts not only between the Indian State and the people but also between different states such as Arunachal Pradesh and Assam. The cases of resistance between the people and the state and between different agencies within the state to uranium extraction from Meghalaya and oil extraction from Rohomoria in Dibrugarh district of Assam are relevant here. Further, issues of land acquisition and displacement are caused while undertaking development programmes and must be given adequate attention. In a society in which capitalist relations of production are not dominant, resource means people's resource since the ownership of the State is not absolute (Chakraborty 2012).

Significantly, the Vision 2020 document makes no mention of the much-debated AFSPA which has been operating in the North-East for long. McDuie-Ra (2009) provides insights into the impact of this so called 'law' on the North-East.

Contestation in the North-East has taken multiple forms such as (i) armed opposition to the Indian state, (ii) violence against migrants, (iii) movements for separate federal states and autonomous units, (iv) demands for more funds from the Central government, and (v) politically generated inter-ethnic conflicts, and so on. AFSPA, operating in the region for over 50 years, provides the basic environment in which the conflicts take place. The only limited changes made in the Act relate to who can impose the law and how long a detained person can be held. The Act provides immunity to the armed forces deployed in the region for surveillance over the people at large. It constitutes de facto martial law and affects relations between (i) soldiers and civilians, (ii) Central and state governments, (iii) industrial estates and its employees, (iv) civil society and government, and (v) India and its neighbouring countries. It aggravates the culture of identity politics in the region and puts counter-insurgency at the heart of planning and keeps the development programmes in the hands of the Central government.

In August 1958, a law was enacted by Parliament (with only Birsa Munda, the tribal MP from Bihar, dissenting) to apply to the hill areas of Assam, especially the Naga Hills and the then Union Territory of Manipur (both now full-fledged states) in order to assist them in the fight against insurgents. The law has been applied in other states as well, such as Jammu and Kashmir (J&K) and Punjab. Since Partition in 1947, the North-East is almost completely cut off from the rest of India, joined only by a narrow corridor at Siliguri in West Bengal. Centred on the Brahmaputra and Barak river valleys, and consisting of eight states sharing borders with Bangladesh, Bhutan, Myanmar, China, and Nepal, the region's various ethnicities have links to South-east Asia and the greater Himalayas. During the colonial era the hill tracts with several less advanced tribes were administered separately and classified as 'excluded' or 'partially excluded', preventing the intrusion of people from the plains to these sensitive areas. Colonial tea and oil interests were located in the Brahmaputra valley. After Independence, the politics of assimilation and integration, most notably in the Naga Hills and Manipur, provoked a violent response with separatist tendencies and called for a perceived need to impose AFSPA with special provisions for ensuring complete immunity to the armed forces in their dealings with civil society and armed opposition groups.

Section 4a of the Act allows 'any commissioned officer, warrant officer, non-commissioned officer, or any other person of equivalent rank in the armed forces' to fire 'even to the causing of death' upon any person acting in contravention of any law or order, any person carrying weapons or anything capable of being used as a weapon, or to prohibit the assembly of more than five people.

Section 4c allows armed forces personnel to arrest without warrant and with any necessary force 'any person who has committed a cognisable offence'.

Section 4d allows armed forces personnel to 'enter and search premises without warrant and to make "any such arrest"'.

Section 5 instructs that the arrested person be handed over to the police with the 'least possible delay' (amended to '24 hours' in 1997).

Section 6 prohibits prosecution of any person in respect of anything done in the exercise of the powers conferred in this Act. AFSPA applies to any area declared 'disturbed' by the Central or state government, the status of which is to be reviewed every six months.

A 1972 amendment provided that the Central government, without consulting the state government, could declare any state or part thereof 'disturbed'. Unlike in 1958, this time there was no debate in Parliament even though the Act covers more than 7 per cent of India's population and more than 7.5 per cent of the land area of the country. The status is not open to judicial review nor can it be contested by state governments (SAHRDC 1995). As of 2008, much of the North-East was designated 'disturbed' including the areas of Arunachal Pradesh bordering Assam, the entire state of Manipur (the Imphal valley was excluded recently), areas of Meghalaya bordering Assam, the entire state of Nagaland and the hill areas of Tripura (HRW 2008, 8–14). In this situation, militant groups appear to have flourished and even grown in numbers since the imposition of AFSPA. Official sources argue this justifies the continuance of the Act but others say that the continuance of the Act has led to the growth in the number of militant groups.

Looking back, it appears that after the Chinese intrusion into the North-East in 1962 and the already present secessionist tendencies in the Naga Hills and Manipur (and later Assam), the main preoccupation of the policy makers has been that of not just maintaining law and order but also checking secessionism in the region. This is what has called for the imposition of AFSPA and the use of the army and central paramilitary forces in the region. The fear of secessionism and fear over the role of hostile neighbours has to be removed before AFSPA can be revoked!

Since 1990s, several international human rights organisations, including the UN High Commissioner for Human Rights (UNHCHR), have protested against the serious violation of human rights by AFSPA and appealed to the Government of India to revoke it. However, AFSPA is only one of the many laws that acts against human rights. There are several others which have been discussed at length (Haragopal and Jagannatham 2009). The Reddy Committee which reviewed the imposition of AFSPA after the killing of Thangjam Manorama of Manipur in suspicious circumstances, recommended repeal of the Act but said that its basic provisions be incorporated into the Unlawful Activities (Prevention) Act, 2004 (UAPA), to make it appear less discriminatory as compared to people in the rest of the country! The recommendation has not yet been accepted presumably because of opposition from AR, the main central agency concerned with security in the North-East. AFSPA thus continues to provide a framework for military occupation in the North-East and inevitable militarisation of daily life in the region causing huge psychological burden on ordinary people. Insurgency in Manipur appears to have become a hugely beneficial proposition to politicians, bureaucrats, and middlemen who milk the Central government of enormous funds. The simple solution is one of sitting down and talking to the insurgent leaders and listening to their problems.

The impact of state violence and counter-violence from armed opposition groups on women has been serious. Women are 'routinely questioned and exposed to sexual harassment' (Chenoy 2002, 132). A study of women in armed conflict situations in the North-East (Srikala and Goswami 2005) identifies several categories of women who are affected: women relatives of armed activists, women relatives of state armed forces, women militants or combatants, women as shelter providers, women as victims of sexual and physical abuse, and women as peace negotiators and activists. The argument is that in militarised societies, even in locations where actual armed conflict is minimal, violence against women is far higher than in non-militarised societies. McDuie-Ra (2007) found that this was true even in respect of Meghalaya with its matriarchal society. Race and gender intersect violence and harassment directed at women, especially by non-tribal members of the armed forces. Obviously in all these cases women include children as well when it comes to harassment and ill-treatment. Another study (Gaikwad 2009) examines the naked protest by the Meira Paibis (torch bearers) in front of AR headquarters against the rape and killing of Thangjam Manorama in 2004 and in support of the on-going 12-year long protest fast by Irom Sharmila Chanu demanding the removal of AFSPA from Manipur as also to explore novel methods of struggle adopted by women in Manipur caught between a violent State and an equally violent armed opposition groups.

Another study by Haksar and Hongray (2011) provides a case study on army rule in north-east India. It focuses on the torture and violence inflicted on ordinary people by AR during a counter-insurgency operation code named 'Operation Bluebird' in 1987 in Oinam and neighbouring villages of Senapati district of Manipur. This was the response of the army to a violent attack on the local AR camp and arms seizure by an armed insurgent group.

The North-East Vision 2020 document indicates the move towards a participatory model of development by India by involving the region in its economic and other engagements with the countries of south-east Asia. The approach is important and relevant but the insistence on sticking to AFSPA could prove an impediment in shaking off the resistance of the people of the region to any attempts to promote happy relations with the Government of India.

In 1947 the princely states of Manipur and Tripura remained separated, and were later integrated into India in 1949. The rest of the region constituted the state of Assam. In 1954, the North East Frontier Agency (NEFA) was created in what is now Arunachal Pradesh, the northern border of which is contested by China. Meghalaya state was carved out of Assam by the North-Eastern Areas (Reorganisation) Act, 1971. The Act also transformed Manipur and Tripura from Union Territories to full-fledged states. Nagaland state had been carved out of Assam by the State of Nagaland Act, 1962 and Mizoram state by the State of Mizoram Act, 1986. Arunachal Pradesh state was created by the State of Arunachal Pradesh Act, 1986. During the colonial period, the British had declared some interior tribal areas in the region 'restricted' or 'partially restricted' areas in order to protect their less advanced and 'pre-modern' tribal populations from intrusion by more advanced and exploitative elements of the Indian 'mainstream'.

The princely states of Manipur and Tripura did not have the administrative and political arrangements which the rest of the country had experienced during the colonial period. These came into existence in these states only after incorporation into India. Both states have significant tribal populations (approximately 27 and 31 per cent, respectively in Manipur and Tripura as per 2011 Census). Strangely, the dominant Meitei community in Manipur was included in the Other Backward Classes (OBCs) of the Indian Constitution, which has left the affected community unhappy. Inter-community relations in Manipur, with Meiteis as majority community, were not a big issue till recently. Tripura was, however, a tribal majority state which was steadily reduced to a tribal minority state on account of the voluntary and involuntary migration of Bengali Hindus and Muslims from East Bengal (now Bangladesh) giving rise to serious tensions.

The states of Mizoram, Meghalaya, Nagaland, and Arunachal Pradesh, once part of Assam, are tribal majority states, although increasingly subject to non-tribal immigration from outside. Assam, the largest state in the North-East with a non-tribal majority, has a significant number of different tribal people living there.

All the specificities of each state need to be taken into account while conducting research and policy studies by official agencies to make appropriate recommendations in a balanced manner.

In this context, the Jeevan Reddy Committee report (2005) on AFSPA needs to be examined since it affects the welfare of the local population and the implementation of the priorities of 'North East India: Vision 2020' policy document.

The Jeeven Reddy Committee was set up in the wake of the rape and murder of a young woman Thangjam Manorama in 2004 allegedly by AR soldiers. The public believes that Manorama was innocent but AR have maintained that she was a dangerous underground militant! Even if their contention were right, her extrajudicial execution was illegal.

The Committee consisted of four male members Justice B.P. Jeevan Reddy, Dr S.B. Nakade, P.P. Srivastava of NEC, General V.R. Raghavan, and journalist Sanjoy Hazarika, but no woman. The non-inclusion of a woman was significant in the light of the increasing violence against women in the region as documented in official reports (GOI 2002). From the report it seems clear that the setting up of the Committee was no more than a sleight of hand or prestidigitation.

The core of the report is in Part IV, Recommendations, and Part V, Suggestions to Amendments to the Unlawful Activities (Prevention) Act (UAPA), 1967. The report admits that AFSPA had become a 'symbol of oppression, an object of hate and an instrument of discrimination and highhandedness'. It, however, contradicts itself when it says that there was an overwhelming opinion in the region that the army should stay but the Act should go! At the same time, the army has made it abundantly clear that they cannot work in the region without AFSPA! Therefore, the Committee recommends that the discriminatory and oppressive provisions of the Act should be incorporated into UAPA. The 'grievance cells' recommended by the Committee are dominated by security officials, which does not have credibility in the public eye. However, the report was not implemented and remains confined to the dark rooms of MHA! Though never made public, a reliable copy is available in the public domain.

Much discussion has taken place as to why the Government of India would not repeal AFSPA. The basic reason appears to be the concern over 'national security' and the refusal of the army to work in the region without the powerful instrument provided by the Act in dealing with the recalcitrant population. This approach is only aggravating the alienation of the public in the region.

The healing process in the North-East, examined in an excellent recent study (Mahanta 2013), may like to learn from the experience of civil society activists in the south Indian state of Andhra Pradesh. They set up and participated as members of the Concerned Citizens' Committee (CCC) to resolve the conflict between the state and the Maoists (1997–2004). The Maoists in India are similar to militant groups in the North-East and the south Indian experience, with due modifications, may be helpful in the region in exploring the possibilities of conflict resolution. In order to be successful, the experience must be painstakingly replicated from the bottom up by civil society activists in every state of the North-East because the causes of conflict differ from state to state.

CCC reports constitute a meticulously documented civil society effort to engage the State and the Maoists simultaneously. In its final report in 2006, CCC noted that the 'reform-led market oriented growth' had led to processes of exclusion of vast masses. A small segment in power perceived any mass mobilisation against the existing order as a serious security threat. In mid-2000s, the reform agenda became more aggressive than before with little scope for imaginative state intervention. This led to the CPI (Maoist) upping the ante in the states of Chhattisgarh, Orissa, Jharkhand, and West Bengal. The CCC viewed violence as arising from a 'political culture that dispensed with accountability and deepened impunity' and said its agenda was about yielding democratic space to expanding 'possibilities for political assertion by ordinary people. It was as much about restoration of rule of law as about urging a mature and humanised and accountable revolutionary praxis' (Maringanti 2010).

Another study (Wallace 2007) states that even after the conflict is eventually resolved, the consequences of the violence and the wounds inflicted on the human survivors and the national psyche need to be healed and a reasonable degree of closure achieved so that the patterns of political violence and terrorism do not recur. He stresses the need for institutionalising efforts to attempt a healing process for societies such as India. 'Closure' should be clearly identified as a core element during periods of political violence focusing on institutionalising human rights, especially for the state, but also for the anti-state political movement. Reconciliation is an obvious element of 'closure'. So are transparency and justice. 'Closure' should include judicial measures ranging from war crime tribunals to informal village-level trials. The major achievement of 'closure' would be transparency. Setting out the facts, opening whatever records are available, and attempting honestly to answer the questions of victims provide a major impetus to healing. It promotes understanding as a first step to some degree of justice and the possibility of forgiveness and reconciliation. Transparency may be the lasting result, a willingness to live with the truth. In political violence, excessive and clandestine means are sometimes used. Similarly, because of security concerns the state often becomes a mirror image of terrorist movement, holding it necessary to use means that are illegal according to the Geneva Convention. Recent developments in Sri Lanka are a good example of what can happen (Wallace 2007). However, some studies do exist in India, which document reconciliation at the grassroots level involving civil society participation following the violence, such as in Gujarat in 2002 (Oommen 2008).

Peace building in the North-East is a complex process and must be accomplished in ways other than 'pacification' through military and paramilitary means as has largely been the case in the region.

shall be made over to the officer in charge of the nearest police station with the least possible delay together with a report of the circumstance occasioning the arrest.

6. **Protection to Persons Acting under this Act**
   No prosecution, suit or other legal proceeding shall be instituted except with previous sanction of the Central Government against any person in respect of anything done or purported to be done in exercise of powers conferred by this Act.

7. **Repeals and Savings**
   a. The Armed Forces (Assam and Manipur) Special Powers Ordinance 1958 is hereby repealed.
   b. Notwithstanding such repeal, anything done or any action taken under the said ordinance shall be deemed to have been done or taken under this Act, as if this Act had commenced on the 22nd day of May 1958.

The Armed Forces (Assam and Manipur) Special Powers (Amendment) Act, 1972 – An Act to Amend the Armed Forces (Assam and Manipur) Special Powers Act, 1958.

Be it enacted by Parliament in the Twenty-third Year of the Republic of India as follows:

1. This Act may be called the Armed Forces (Assam and Manipur) Special Powers (Amendment) Act, 1972.
2. In the Armed Forces (Assam and Manipur) Special Powers Act, 1958 (hereinafter referred to as the principal Act) in the long title, for the word "in the State of Assam and the Union Territory of Manipur", the words "in the States of Assam, Manipur, Meghalaya, Nagaland and Tripura and Union Territories of Arunachal Pradesh and Mizoram" shall be substituted.

3. In section 1 of the principal Act,
   - In sub-section (1) for the words, brackets and figures "the Armed Forces (Assam and Manipur) Special Powers Act, 1958", the words, brackets and figures "the Armed Forces (Special Powers) Act, 1958" shall be substituted:
   - For sub-section (2) the following sub-section shall be substituted namely:
   - (2) It extends to the whole of the States of Assam, Manipur, Meghalaya, Nagaland and Tripura and the Union Territories of Arunachal Pradesh and Mizoram.
4. For section 3 of the principal Act, the following section shall be substituted, namely: (3) If in relation to any State or Union Territory to which this act extends, the Governor of the State or the Administrator of the Union Territory, as the case may be, is of the opinion that it is in such a disturbed or dangerous condition that the use of Armed Forces in aid of the civil power is necessary, the Governor of the State or the Administrator of the Union Territory or the Central Government, as the case may be, may by notification in the official Gazette, declare the whole or such part of such state or Union Territory to be a disturbed area.

As from the commencement of this Act, the principal Act, as extended by notification of the Government of India in the Ministry of Home Affairs No GSR 1970, dated the 25th November, shall cease to operate in the State of Tripura.

Corrected on 21 November 2012
(*Source*: Haksar and Hongray 2011, 343–48)

References

- Barbora, S. 2006. 'Rethinking India's Counter-insurgency Campaign in the Northeast'. *Economic and Political Weekly* 2 September: 3205–12.

- Chakraborty, N. 2012. *North East Vision 2020: A Reality Check.* Mimeo. Institute of Development Studies Kolkata (IDSK), Salt Lake, Kolkata.
- Chenoy, A. 2002. *Militarism and Women in South Asia.* New Delhi: Kali for Women.
- Choudhury, S. in K.S. Aggarwal (ed.). 1999. *Dynamics of Identity and Inter-group Relations in the North-East India.* Indian Institute of Advanced Study, Shimla.
- Fernandes, W. 2004. 'Limits of Law and Order Approach to the North East'. *Economic and Political Weekly* 16 October.
- Gaikwad, N. 2009. 'Revolting Bodies: Hysterical State: Women Protesting the Armed Forces (Special Powers) Act, 1958'. *Contemporary South Asia* 17 (3): 299–311.
- GOI. 2002. *India Human Development Report.* Planning Commission, Government of India.
- GOI. 2008a. *Capacity Building for Conflict Resolution: Friction to Fusion.* Seventh Report. Second Administrative Reforms Commission.
- GOI. 2008b. *Report of the Experts Group on Development Challenges in Extremist Affected Areas.* Planning Commission, Government of India.
- GOI. 2008c. *North East Vision, 2020.* Ministry for the Development of the North-Eastern Region, New Delhi.
- Haksar, Nandita and S. Hongray. 2011. *The Judgement that Never Came: Army Rule in North.* New Delhi: Chicken Neck Publishers.
- Haragopal, G. and B. Jagannatham. 2009. 'Terrorism and Human Rights: Indian Experience with Repressive Laws'. *Economic and Political Weekly* 44(28).
- HRW. 2008. 'Getting Away with Murder: Fifty Years of Armed Forces (Special Powers) Act, 1958'. New York: Human Rights Watch.
- ———. 2009. *Broken System: Dysfunction, Abuse and Impunity in the Indian Police.* New York: Human Rights Watch.
- Kikon, Dolly. 2009. 'The Predicament of Justice: Fifty Years of AFSPA in India'. *Contemporary Asia.* 17(3): 271–82.
- Maringanti, Anant. 2010. 'Talks between the Maoists and the State:

Learning from the Andhra Experience'. *Economic and Political Weekly* 21 August.

- Mahanta, Nani Gopal. 2013. *Confronting the State: ULFA's Quest for Sovereignty.* New Delhi: Sage Publications.
- McDuie-Ra. 2007. 'Anti-development or Identity Crisis: Misreading Civil Society in Meghalaya, India'. *Asian Ethnicity* 8(1): 43–59.
- ———. 2009. 'Vision 2020 or Re-vision, 1958: The Contradictory Politics of Counter-insurgency in India's Regional Engagement'. *Contemporary South Asia* 17(3) September 2009: 313–30.
- Mukherjee, P. 2007. 'India's "Look East" Policy'. *Dialogue* 9(1) July–September.
- Mullik, B.N. 1972. *My Years with Nehru.* New Delhi: Allied Publishers.
- Navlakha, G. 2011. 'On Ending the War against Our Own People'. *Economic and Political Weekly* 19 February.
- Oommen, T.K. 2008. *Reconciliation in Post-Godhra Gujarat: The Role of Civil Society.* New Delhi: Pearson–Longman.
- Phanjoubam, P. 2007. 'Look East Policy: Beyond Trade and Commerce for North East'. *Dialogue* 9(1) July–September.
- Rustomji, Nari. 1983. *Imperilled Frontiers.* New Delhi: Oxford University Press.
- SAHRDC. 1995. *AFSPA: A Study in National Security Tyranny.* South Asia Human Rights Documentation Centre.
- Srikala, N.G. and R. Goswami. 2005. *Women in Armed Conflict Situations.* Guwahati: North East Network.
- Srinivasavaradan, T.C.A. 1992. *The Federal Concept: The Indian Experience.* New Delhi: Allied Publishers.
- Subramanian, K.S. 2007. *Political Violence and the Police in India.* New Delhi: Sage Publications.
- ———. 2010. 'State Response to Maoist Violence: A Critical Assessment'. *Economic and Political Weekly* August 7.
- Wallace, Paul. 2007. 'A Grassroots Approach to Healing Terrorism', in *Democracy and Counter-terrorism: Lessons from the Past.* Washington, D.C.: US Institute of Peace.

SECURITY

Hydropower Projects: Threat to Environmental Security in the North-East

Neeraj Vagholikar and Partha J. Das

The North-East is identified as India's 'future power house'. At least 168 large hydroelectric projects are set to alter the riverscape significantly. Large dams are emerging as a major issue of conflict in the region. Although the current scale of dam-related developments far outstrips anything which took place in the past, the region has been no stranger to dam-related conflicts. The Kaptai dam, built in the Chittagong Hill Tracts (now in Bangladesh) in the 1960s, submerged the traditional homelands of the Hajong and Chakma indigenous communities and forced them to migrate to the North-East leading to serious conflicts between the refugees and local communities in Arunachal Pradesh.

In the 1970s, the Gumti dam in Tripura submerged large tracts of arable land in the Raima valley and displaced the local tribal population leading to tribal unrest. The Loktak hydroelectric project impacted the wetland ecology of Loktak lake in Manipur in the 1980s, seriously affecting the habitat of the endangered Sangai (brow-antlered deer) and the livelihoods of local people. The impending loss of home, land, and livelihood has led to many years of opposition to Pagladiya project in Assam and Tipaimukh project in Manipur on the Barak river.

More recently, major conflicts in Assam and Arunachal Pradesh have emerged over individual and cumulative impacts of over 100 dams planned in upstream Arunachal. Dam-induced floods from hydroelectric projects such as the 405 MW Ranganadi hydroelectric project in Arunachal Pradesh and people's strong opposition to the 2000 MW Lower Subansiri hydroelectric project under construction on the Assam–Arunachal Pradesh border have triggered a major political debate on the downstream impacts of dams in the region.

Meanwhile, in the uplands of Sikkim and Arunachal, minority indigenous communities such as Lepchas and Idu Mishmis have expressed concern over the impacts of multiple mega power projects in their homelands. The large dams' juggernaut promises to be the biggest 'development' intervention in this ecologically and geologically fragile, seismically active, and culturally sensitive region in the coming days.

The Region

North-east India, consisting of the eight states of Assam, Arunachal Pradesh, Manipur, Meghalaya, Mizoram, Nagaland, Tripura, and Sikkim, is known for its biological and cultural diversity and the unique Brahmaputra and Barak river systems. While the eight states are indeed collectively referred to as the North-East, there is substantial diversity within the region even as far as political and socio-economic issues are concerned, both historically and in contemporary times.

The region is rich in biodiversity and is home to important wildlife species such as rhino, elephant, tiger, wild water buffalo, pygmy hog, and Gangetic river dolphin. Three out of 34 biodiversity hotspots identified globally in the Himalayas, Indo–Myanmar, Western Ghats, and Sri Lanka cover parts of India. The North-East is traversed by the first two and in 8 per cent of the country's geographical area it also houses 21 per cent of important bird sanctuaries in India, identified as per international criteria. It is an area which is still poorly documented. In recent years biologists have discovered new species and extended known ranges of existing ones in the region. This is not just restricted to smaller life forms, but includes large mammals such as primates, discovery of which is rare these days, an indication of how unexplored the region is. The North-East also has a high level of endemism (plant and animal species found nowhere else).

Brahmaputra is one of the world's largest rivers, with a drainage basin of 5,80,000 sq. km, 33 per cent of which is in India. It originates in the great glacier mass of Chema-Yung-Dung in the Kailas range of southern Tibet at an elevation of 5,300 m. It traverses 1,625 km through Chinese territory, 918 km through India, and a final stretch of 337 km through Bangladesh before joining the Bay of Bengal through a joint channel with the Ganga. A unique river, it drains such diverse environments as the cold dry plateau of Tibet, the rain-drenched Himalayan slopes, the landlocked alluvial plains of Assam and the vast deltaic lowlands of Bangladesh. An extremely dominant monsoon and a unique physiographic setting, fragile geological base, active seismo-tectonic instability, together with anthropogenic factors, have moulded Brahmaputra into one of the world's most intriguing and gigantic river systems. The dramatic reduction in the slope of the Brahmaputra as it cascades through one of the world's deepest gorges in the Himalayas before flowing into the Assam plains explains the sudden dissipation of the enormous energy locked in it and the resultant unloading of large amounts of sediments in the valley downstream. The river carries the second largest sediment yield in the world, while it ranks fourth in terms of water discharge.

In the course of its 2,880 km journey to the Bay of Bengal, Brahmaputra receives as many as 22 major tributaries in Tibet, 33 in India, and three in Bangladesh. Many of the north bank tributaries are of Himalayan origin, fed by glaciers in their upper reaches, such as Subansiri, Jia Bharali (Kameng), and Manas. Dibang and Lohit are two large tributaries emerging from the extreme eastern flank of the Himalayas, while Jiadhal, Ranganadi, Puthimari, and Pagladiya are some of the major tributaries with sources in the sub-Himalayas, the latter two being in Bhutan. The river system is intricately linked with the floodplain ecology of wetlands (*beels*) and grasslands in the Brahmaputra valley. For example, these linkages are evident in the world-renowned ecosystems such as the Kaziranga National Park in Assam. Due to the colliding Eurasian (Chinese) and Indian tectonic plates, the Brahmaputra valley and its adjoining hill ranges are seismically very unstable and the region has seen some major earthquakes.

The other major river basin in north-east India is the Barak. This river originates in Manipur and the upper Barak catchment area extends over almost the entire north, north-western, western, and south-western portion of the state. The middle course of the river lies in the plains of Cachar in southern Assam, while the lower, deltaic course in Bangladesh. Both the Brahmaputra and the Barak river systems are also the lifeline for livelihoods such as fishing and agriculture of local communities in their respective floodplains.

The region is home to diverse indigenous communities, mostly dependent on natural resource-based livelihoods. This diversity of communities comes with unique socio-cultural, agro-ecological and land-holding systems (such as different forms of community control over forests in various parts of the region). By the late 19th century, tea and other business had brought massive demographic and economic changes to undivided Assam. But the experience was varied across the region. For example, the area that would later become Arunachal Pradesh was relatively isolated from such changes. In 1875, the British established the 'inner line'—a demarcation between the Assamese plains and the mountains through which nobody could pass without a permit. This restriction and the geography of the region kept Arunachal Pradesh isolated from upheavals, such as conversion of massive stretches of land into privately owned tea gardens, as seen in Assam.

The region today is marked by socio-political complexities, which include struggles for political autonomy and associated armed conflicts. The Indian constitution has attempted to deal with the North-East's unique nature by establishing a system of administration that differs from the rest of the country. The Sixth Schedule and other constitutional provisions relevant to the North-East offer different degrees of autonomy and self-management (including natural resource management) to indigenous communities. Despite this, there seems to be little opportunity for them to participate in decisions related to large developmental projects. Faced with a multitude of challenges, the region is currently charting a course for 'development'. Establishing large hydel projects for power production and export is part of the government's development plan.

North-East Power Surge

In 2001 the Central Electricity Authority (CEA) studied the preliminary ranking of the hydroelectric potential of various river basins in the country. The Brahmaputra basin was ranked high and 168 projects with a total installed capacity of 63,328 MW were identified. The 'future powerhouse' tag has been proactively used for the region since the North-East Business Summit in Mumbai in July 2002. The 50,000 MW hydro initiative launched by the Ministry of Power in 2003 also focuses on the North-East. The Pasighat Proclamation on Power adopted in January 2007 at the North-East Council's Sectoral Summit on the Power Sector identifies the region's hydropower potential as one of the priority areas to contribute to the country's energy security.

The push for large hydropower projects in the North-East was primarily a process driven by the Central Government till hydropower policies were gradually liberalised and private sector participation was allowed. While Sikkim kick-started this process in the North-East in 2001–02, it gathered momentum across the region by 2005. Arunachal Pradesh and Sikkim were at the forefront of the initiative to sign multiple Memoranda of Understanding/Agreement (MoUs/MoAs) with power developers. Meghalaya, Manipur, Mizoram, and

Nagaland too have seen some action in this direction. Assam and Tripura are smaller players in hydropower because of their topography.

In May 2008, the then Union Minister of State for Power, Jairam Ramesh, raised concern about the 'MoU virus' affecting states like Arunachal Pradesh and Sikkim. He was referring to the rapid pace at which MoUs or MoAs were being signed by these governments with hydropower companies, particularly in the private sector. Till October 2010, the government of Arunachal Pradesh had already allotted 132 projects to companies in the private and public sectors for a total installed capacity of 40,140.5 MW. About 120 of these projects involved private sector. Each of these agreements has been followed by disbursement of huge monetary advances from project developers at the time of inking the deal. This was done before any public consultations, preparation of detailed project reports (DPRs) or even receipt of mandatory clearances!

This process of signing MoUs, where monetary advances are paid upfront, greatly compromises the manner in which subsequent clearances take place as such projects are considered a *fait accompli* by both the developer and the state government. Moreover, it leaves no room for an assessment of options for development planning in areas where these projects are coming up. The Comptroller and Auditor General (CAG) of India, the supreme audit institution in the country, has, in the performance audit for 2008–09 for the state of Sikkim, highlighted serious concerns about the manner in which projects have been handed out to some private hydropower players. While the Meghalaya Legislative Assembly has seen a debate and conducted an enquiry on the manner in which projects had been allotted to private sector in the state, the Assam Legislative Assembly has debated the implications of the dams' juggernaut in upstream Arunachal Pradesh. In Arunachal Pradesh too, local affected communities, civil society groups, the media, and opposition political parties have repeatedly raised serious concerns about the process of rapidly allotting projects to power developers without any public consultation.

Despite the concern raised by a central minister about the 'MoU virus', the Central Government has cleared these projects ignoring important questions. At least two dozen large hydroelectric projects have got the final environmental clearance in the North-East. Apart from the seven large hydroelectric projects in Arunachal Pradesh which have already received final environmental clearance, at least 50 more have received the first stage of environmental clearance for carrying out pre-construction activities. While all pre-construction clearances do not necessarily translate into final clearances, existing experience shows that the Ministry of Environment and Forests (MoEF) grants final environmental clearance to over 95 per cent of all projects, the environmental and social impacts of which it reviews.

The government and the proponents of large dams in the region paint a win-win picture such as exploiting the country's largest perennial water system to produce large amount of power for the nation; economic benefits for north-eastern states through export of power to other parts of the country; employment generation; less displacement of local communities as compared to other projects elsewhere in the country; promise of the dams and private capital changing the perceived 'lack of development' scenario of the region forever.

The Environmental Impact Assessment (EIA) Farce

Considering the unique features of the region and the scale of intervention planned, it is critical that the social and environmental impacts are critically studied before deciding on the feasibility of these projects. Large hydroelectric projects need to obtain mandatory 'environmental clearance' from MoEF to evaluate their viability on environmental and social grounds. Based on the location, they might also need other clearances such as 'forest clearance' from MoEF and approval from the standing committee of the National Board for Wildlife (NBWL) for locations inside or within 10 km radius of wildlife protected areas (PAs). A key feature of the environmental clearance process is the EIA report, which is critical in aiding the decision-making. It may be noted that this is the only study under the current clearance mechanisms to include a mandatory component on social impact assessment (SIA).

What about the quality of these EIA reports for dams in north-east India? Let us look at the biodiversity aspects of some EIA reports. Dr Anwaruddin Choudhury, renowned naturalist from north-east India, has examined the EIA reports of at least five large hydroelectric projects—Kameng, Lower Subansiri, Middle Siang, Tipaimukh, and Dibang—and finds them all poor on wildlife aspects. A common feature of his introductory comments on these reports is '(It) contains innumerable (instances of) incorrect data, unverified and superfluous statements, and above all reveals the casual approach,' referring to power companies and EIA consultants. Dr Choudhury says, 'It is shocking that mega hydel projects in the North-East are being granted clearances based on such reports. How can we decide the fate of some of the country's most important wildlife habitats based on sub-standard impact assessment studies?'

Discrepancies in Some EIA Reports

The EIA report for the 1,000 MW Siyom project lists five bird species in an area which has over 300. Even this short list has one which is non-existent.

The EIA report for the 600 MW Kameng project reclassifies carnivores animals such as the red panda, pangolins, and porcupines as herbivores.

The EIA report for the 2,000 MW Lower Subansiri project lists 55 species of fish in a river which has at least 156 and reports an area called the 'Arctic' in the eastern Himalayas.

But these days citizens' groups are getting cynical and increasingly reluctant to send their comments to the government on poor EIA reports. That is because necessary additional and credible studies are rarely asked for by authorities. On the contrary, the reports are sanitised by developers based on the comments received, to weed out problematic portions, and the projects conveniently granted clearance.

In some cases additional rapid EIAs have been asked for, which prove to be entirely inadequate. In the Lower Subansiri project on the Assam–Arunachal Pradesh border, the Zoological Survey of India (ZSI) spent six days doing an additional study and then made surprising statements such as, 'The long and vast water body thus created by the reservoir will be happy haunt for aquatic creatures.' It is well known that native aquatic species, whose habitats are fast-flowing rivers, do not find the still waters of a reservoir a 'happy haunt'! While reservoirs may benefit exotic species that are introduced for fisheries, such introduction has very often proved to be detrimental to the native species. It is a matter of serious concern that reputed government institutions such as ZSI have given such poor reports. While biodiversity was used as an indicator in the above examples, the reports have been found to be poor in many social and environmental aspects in general. In some cases MoEF has indeed asked for additional detailed studies when EIAs were found to be poor, but often they have been post-clearance studies! There is little logic in first clearing the way for destruction of wildlife habitats and then doing a detailed assessment as a formality after project work and environmental destruction is well under way.

Another trend has been to grant clearances to projects that destroy sensitive wildlife habitat based on poor assessments, and then claim to compensate the losses by asking for other areas to be protected. While appropriate compensatory mechanisms may be relevant in some cases, they cannot substitute a sound decision-making process based on comprehensive environmental and social impact assessment. The main problem in current environmental decision-making process is that virtually every project is treated a *fait accompli* both by the expert committees appraising these projects and the regulatory authorities concerned. This subverts the possibility of a proper environmental decision-making process.

Dulal Goswami, environmental scientist and renowned expert on the Brahmaputra river basin says

> The geophysical nature of the Brahmaputra river basin is fragile and dynamic. The scientific knowledge base on the river system is currently very poor, for example, on aspects such as sedimentation and hydrology which are linked to the economic life of the project. This needs to be strengthened urgently; more so in the light of emerging threats from climate change. Without the availability of comprehensive information, how can we determine the long-term viability of projects in this region? The wisdom of such public policy has to be questioned. Economic viability apart, the mega-projects planned come with tremendous ecological and social costs which are unacceptable.

Underestimating Social Impacts

One of the major arguments put forward in New Delhi to 'sell' large hydroelectric projects in the North-East is that there is relatively 'small displacement' by submergence as compared to that in other parts of the country and, therefore, these projects are benign. But a careful perusal of the ground situation indicates that displacement, particularly of livelihoods and rights, is grossly underestimated. Azing Pertin of the Siang Peoples Forum in Arunachal Pradesh says

> Since our state is hilly, there is very little land where permanent cultivation is possible. Virtually all our available arable lands will be submerged by the 2700 MW Lower Siang project

> in the affected area in the Siang Valley. The magnitude of impact has to be understood keeping this context in mind. It is misleading to argue that the land being lost is a small percentage of the total area of the district or state and wrongly assume that the project is benign.

The impacts of dams on resources under common use, such as pasture lands, vital to livelihoods of local communities, is also a major missing link in impact assessment of projects. Shifting agriculture (*jhum*) is a dominant traditional land use in the hills of north-east India which plays an important role in the livelihoods of people, maintaining agricultural biodiversity and providing food security. Increasing pressures on land have resulted in the shortening of *jhum* cycle (the gap between two cropping phases), thus impacting the ecological viability of this farming system. The submergence of land by hydel projects will further shorten the *jhum* cycle and enhance the pressure on the surrounding areas, thus affecting the environment and livelihoods of *jhum*-dependent communities over a much larger landscape. In addition to the submergence, land use restrictions will apply in the catchment area of the reservoir as per mandatory norms to reduce siltation and to increase the life of the reservoir. Further, compensatory mechanisms required as per forest laws to offset the loss of forests due to the project also lead to protection of other areas, affecting community access to land and resources. Take, for example, the conversion of unclassified state forests in Arunachal Pradesh, which allow more access and control by local communities, into protected forests, with greater state control. The impacts on rights of local communities in such cases need also to be examined in terms of the Scheduled Tribes and Other Traditional Forest Dwellers (Recognition of Forest Rights) Act, 2006.

Clearly, the impact on local communities is well beyond just the submergence area. However, in the existing planning and decision making process, the social and environmental impacts over the larger landscape due to various aspects described above are not assessed. This is, therefore, not reflected on the decisions on the overall viability of the project.

States such as Arunachal Pradesh are home to small populations of culturally sensitive indigenous communities. Therefore, if the local population (as opposed to the population of the country) is considered, direct and indirect displacement is high. Dr Mite Lingi, Chairman of the Idu Indigenous Peoples Forum, says

> The 'small displacement' argument to sell these projects as being benign needs to be confronted. The entire population of the Idu Mishmi tribe is around 9500 and at least 17 large hydel projects have been planned in our home, the Dibang Valley in Arunachal. As per this faulty argument, little social impact will be indicated even if our entire population were supposedly displaced!

The land in the state has also been customarily delineated between different indigenous communities and clans. Therefore, contrary to popular belief, there is not plenty of land for resettling people in the state, just because the population density is less.

Furthermore, the concerns in states like Arunachal Pradesh and Sikkim are not restricted to displacement. The over two-year long *satyagraha* in Sikkim by affected indigenous communities during June 2007–September 2009 focused on the impacts of hydel projects on Dzongu, the holy land and reserve of the Lepcha tribe. The protests have also received support of the Buddhist monk community in Sikkim, as a sacred landscape stands to be desecrated. Sociologist Vibha Arora says, 'Such protests are not merely on grounds of displacement but that the region's cultural and ethnic traditions are rooted in the river Teesta and its environs.' A major concern in the North-East is the influx of large labour populations from outside the region. Dr Lingi adds

> We have been given constitutional and legal protection, particularly with respect to our land rights and restricted entry of outsiders. These projects are going to require both skilled and unskilled labour which Arunachal Pradesh cannot provide. Seventeen large projects in the Dibang Valley will bring in outside labour, upwards of 1,50,000 people, for long periods, as these are long gestation projects. We are concerned about the demographic changes and other socio-cultural impacts associated with this, as the Idu Mishmis are only 9,500 in number. The development policies are in glaring contradiction to the constitutional and legal protection we have been given.

Despite major movements emerging in the region raising serious concerns about the impacts of dams, it will be misleading to argue that there is universal opposition to hydropower projects across the North-East. In states such as Sikkim, Arunachal Pradesh, and Manipur, there are some among local communities who defend the projects. Monetary gains from sale of land, small contracts during construction and a promise of quicker development of basic infrastructure like roads and bridges is cited as a major motivation. Responding to these arguments, journalist-activist Raju Mimi from Dibang Valley of Arunachal Pradesh says

> We certainly want a bridge across the Lohit river at Dhollaghat. But the government cannot thrust on us some of the world's largest hydropower projects, such as 3,000 MW Dibang and 4,000 MW Etalin, by promising that we will get a bridge in return! What kind of governance is this? We should get the bridge irrespective of whether these hydropower projects come up or not.

While dam related opposition has primarily been seen in Assam, Arunachal Pradesh, Sikkim, and Manipur in recent times, the state of Mizoram saw a major rally against dams in the Sinlung hills in September 2010. Perhaps the first of its kind in the state, the rally was organised by the Sinlung Indigenous Peoples Human Rights Organisation (SIPHRO) and Sinlung Peoples Collective in Aizawl, capital of Mizoram. Their memorandum to the chief minister, also signed by a wide array of civil society groups in the state who participated in the rally, argues that dams are being pushed for the benefit of a few influential individuals in the state who seek to corner the financial gains from compensation and contracts. They claim that in the Serlui B and Tuirial hydropower projects this has already happened. Opposing the plans to extensively dam all big and small rivers in the Singlung hills, they state that the land, rivers, and forests are the backbone of the existence and survival of the Hmar and other indigenous people of the region. A crucial argument they forward is that their very citizenship and democratic rights are integrally embedded with the land, forests, and rivers and these must be safeguarded and protected for all time to come.

We All Live Downstream

A topic of heated debate currently in the North-East is the downstream impacts of dams, often not found in popular discourses on the impacts of dams in the country, primarily influenced by upstream submergence and displacement. When large dams block the flow of a river, they also trap sediments and nutrients vital for the nourishment of downstream plains. They alter the natural flow regimes which drive the ecological processes in the downstream areas. Quite literally they disrupt the connections between the upstream and the downstream, between a river and its floodplain.

A major catalyst to trigger the larger debate on downstream impacts of dams in Assam has been the repeated incidents of dam-induced floods across the state from upstream projects such as the 405 MW Ranganadi project in Arunachal Pradesh in recent years. Downstream impact concerns raised in the North-East include loss of fisheries, changes in *beel* (wetland) ecology in the flood plains, impacts on agriculture on the *chapories* (riverine islands and tracts), impacts on various other livelihoods due to blockage of rivers by dams (e.g. driftwood collection and sand and gravel mining), increased flood vulnerability due to massive boulder extraction from river beds for dam construction and sudden water releases from reservoirs in the monsoons, and dam safety and associated risks in this geologically fragile and seismically active region. The Brahmaputra valley, a thickly populated narrow strip of land surrounded by hills, has woken up to the fact that it is going to be increasingly vulnerable to risks from existing and proposed large dams upstream. This realisation has been significant for a civilisation whose cultural identity—customs, food habits, music, and religious beliefs—is inextricably linked to its river systems.

One of the key issues that has come up is the drastic daily variation in river flows particularly in winter after these dams are commissioned. For example, the average winter (lean season) flow in the Subansiri river is approximately 400 cubic metres per second (cumecs). Both the ecology of the downstream areas and people's use of the riverine tracts in winter is adapted to this 'lean' but relatively uniform flow of water on any particular day (with a gradual variation through the season). *Chapories*, for example, which are exposed and drier in winter are used for both agriculture and cattle grazing purposes, by local communities, and simultaneously by wildlife. After the commissioning of the 2,000 MW Lower Subansiri project, flows in the Subansiri river will fluctuate drastically on a daily basis in winter from 6 cumecs for around 20 hours (when water is being stored behind the dam) to 2,560 cumecs for around 4 hours when water is released for power generation at the time of peak power demand in the evening hours. Thus the river will be starved for 20 hours and then flooded for 4 hours with flows fluctuating between 2 per cent and 600 per cent of normal flows every day.

The flow during peak load water releases in the Subansiri river in winter will be equivalent to average monsoon flows and will cause a 'winter flood' daily drowning drier riverine tracts used both by people and wildlife throughout the winter. The downstream livelihoods and activities likely to be impacted by this unnatural flow fluctuation in the eastern Himalayan rivers include fishing, flood-recession agriculture (such as mustard), river transportation, and livestock rearing in grasslands for dairy-based livelihoods. But downstream communities are yet to be officially acknowledged as project-affected persons due to upstream dams. Flow fluctuations in rivers such as Lohit, Dibang, Siang, and Subansiri will seriously impact breeding grounds of critically endangered grassland birds such as the Bengal Florican, foraging areas of the endangered wild water buffalo, habitat of the endangered Ganges river dolphin and important national parks such as Dibru–Saikhowa and Kaziranga. The natural flow pattern of a river is like its 'heart beat' and alternate starving and flooding of these major rivers on a daily basis is a threat to the ecological and social security of the Brahmaputra floodplains.

Serious concerns have been raised in Assam by a wide spectrum of civil society groups such as through mass movements and students unions on the downstream concerns vis-à-vis the spate of mega dams planned in Arunachal Pradesh. A major focus of conflict has been the 2,000 MW Lower Subansiri project, under construction on the Assam–Arunachal Pradesh border. Downstream agitations by local movements and the All Assam Students' Union (AASU) led to the setting up of an inter-disciplinary expert committee to study the downstream impacts of the project. Interim recommendations were made by this committee in February 2009 to stop work pending completion of the report. But they were ignored by the power company as well as both the state and central governments. In their final report submitted in June 2010 this committee recommended, 'The selected site for the mega dam of the present dimension was not appropriate in such a geologically and seismologically sensitive location ... Therefore, it is recommended not to construct the mega dam in the present site....'

Following a major debate in the Assam Legislative Assembly in July 2009, a House Committee was set up to look at the impacts of dams on downstream Assam. The committee, in its July 2010 report, has categorically endorsed the recommendations of the Expert Committee raising concerns about the Lower Subansiri project. On 12 August, Rajya Sabha saw a lively discussion on the issue in response to a calling attention motion by Birendra Prasad Baishya, a Member of Parliament from Assam. As the follow-up to a meeting held in August 2010 with a delegation led by the Krishak Mukti Sangram Samiti, a major peasants' movement in Assam, union environment minister Jairam Ramesh held a public consultation on the issue in Guwahati on 10 September. Apart from the Brahmaputra valley in Assam, downstream impact debates have also raged in Manipur and in southern Assam, in the Barak valley, downstream of the proposed 1,500 MW Tipaimukh dam. A long battle fought by those affected by the Mapithel dam in Manipur in the Thoubal river basin has forced the state government to conduct a review of the impacts of the project, including in the downstream areas.

Media reports indicate that the Union Environment Minister has communicated to the Prime Minister the concerns raised in the 10 September public consultation in Guwahati. We need to, however, wait and watch whether the Centre responds adequately to the serious concerns raised in the downstream areas of the proposed projects. However, a study of decision-making until now makes one thing amply clear: the Central Government denies a basic fact of nature – that a river flows downstream. This is evident from the terms of reference (ToR) for EIA studies granted by MoEF for at least 50 large hydroelectric projects in Arunachal Pradesh from September 2006 to August 2010. In most cases the 'baseline data' is restricted to only 10 km downstream of the project and the actual 'impact prediction' has been asked to be restricted to an even shorter distance downstream—only between the dam and the powerhouse! There is only one aspect which is mandatory to be studied beyond 10 km downstream in all cases. This is the 'dam break analysis' which predicts the effects of flooding downstream, in case the dam actually collapses. But dam break is not the only downstream risk a dam poses, as indicated earlier. Unfortunately, most detailed downstream studies are only prescribed as post-clearance studies as has been done in the environmental clearance granted to the 1,500 MW Tipaimukh multipurpose project in October 2008 and to the 1,750 MW Demwe Lower project on the Lohit river in February 2010. This clearly indicates that the projects are being treated a *fait accompli* and the clearance processes just a formality. It was only recently that MoEF for the first time prescribed partial downstream impact studies for a few projects before grant of clearance (e.g. 3,000 MW Dibang multipurpose project and 2,700 MW Lower Siang project). But the ToRs in these cases, too, do not ask for comprehensive downstream studies, which should have been the case.

Cumulative Impacts of Dams and Carrying Capacity of River Basins

With multiple dams in each river basin, the issue of cumulative impact of dams has become a crucial issue. The late Nari Rustomji, who served as Assam's chief secretary and Dewan of Sikkim had, through his writings, warned that development inputs into Sikkim needed to be within the absorptive capacity of the region. In 1998, the Expert Appraisal Committee (EAC) on River Valley and Hydroelectric Projects, appointed by MoEF noted Rustomji's observations while examining a proposal for environmental clearance of the 510 MW Teesta hydroelectric project in Sikkim. Since this was one of the multiple large hydroelectric works in the ecologically and culturally sensitive Teesta river basin, the committee recommended a detailed study on the 'carrying capacity' of the river basin before taking a decision. But MoEF granted clearance to the project without such a study being completed in advance. However, one of the conditions for clearance to the project was that 'no other project in Sikkim will be considered for environmental clearance till the carrying capacity study is completed.'

In spite of this self-imposed condition MoEF subsequently granted environmental clearance to at least seven new hydroelectric projects before the study on carrying capacity was finally completed in early 2008. The ministry has thus violated its own mandatory condition. Sikkimese civil society groups such as the Affected Citizens of Teesta (ACT) are disappointed that a golden opportunity has been lost. There was hope that the carrying capacity study process would enable a comprehensive assessment of the cumulative impact of several proposed hydroelectric projects and a serious options-assessment for ecologically and culturally sensitive development in the Teesta river basin. But MoEF has continued granting clearance to one project after another without seriously examining the issue in an holistic manner as per its own mandated condition. After completion of the study in 2008, however, MoEF had declared certain areas in north Sikkim in the Teesta river basin as 'no-go' areas for dams. But this condition too has been recommended for dilution by the EAC in early 2010, threatening to open up the last free-flowing stretches of the Teesta in Sikkim for more dams.

In fact, the National Environmental Appellate Authority (NEAA), a special environmental court, in an April 2007 order has also observed that it feels the need for 'advance cumulative study of series of different dams coming on any river so as to assess the optimum capacity of the water resource giving due consideration to the requirement of the Human beings, Cattle, Ecology/Environment etc.' However, this order has been repeatedly violated by MoEF. Even though level studies have been prescribed for some river basins such as Bichom and Lohit in Arunachal Pradesh, these have been de-linked from clearances to be granted to individual projects. Therefore, project clearance can continue in a business-as-usual manner, without completion of cumulative studies, making it a cosmetic exercise.

In December 2008, the standing committee of the National Board for Wildlife (NBWL) has relaxed conditions for construction of dams in the upstream areas of Subansiri river. This restriction was imposed in May 2003 while granting clearance to the 2,000 MW Lower Subansiri hydroelectric project on the Arunachal Pradesh–Assam border. This relaxation has been effected without consulting Assam, located downstream, and ignoring the demand by some members of the committee to first get an estimate of the cumulative impact of 22 large hydel projects which can potentially come up in the Subansiri river basin, once the restriction has been lifted. The Inter-Ministerial Group (IMG) set up to study and provide recommendations for accelerating hydropower development in the North-East has, in its 2010 report, specifically recommended that MoEF should not hold up environmental clearances pending completion of cumulative impact assessment studies, thus rendering the entire exercise futile.

EAC in its September 2010 meeting has finally opined that a cumulative downstream impact assessment does indeed require to be carried out in Assam to study the impacts of multiple projects in the Brahmaputra river basin. It was, however, silent on the need to stall environmental clearances of individual projects until the study is completed.

People, Development, and Power

In the current situation it seems difficult to bring accountability back to the governance process on these mega-hydel projects in the North-East. The arguments on development and power being used to ride roughshod over some of the country's most important ecological landscapes and the livelihood rights of the people of the region need to be addressed, too.

The argument that these mega-power projects are crucial for India's energy security is a major instrument for subversion of environmental and social issues. This myth needs to be busted. Girish Sant of Prayas Energy Group, a leading organisation working on public interest power sector issues, says

> Development needs increase energy services. But demand forecasts that planners make are usually an overestimate and there is a bias towards centralised large projects to meet this highly inflated demand. This is not the 'least-cost' way of getting the required services. With increasing conflicts over the siting of new power projects, we urgently need an alternative approach towards power sector planning such as Integrated Resource Planning (IRP). Such an approach can have substantial environmental and social benefits as energy services can be delivered with a sizeable reduction in the number of new power plants required by the country. IRP considers a mix of supply side and demand side solutions while giving equal importance to both. It includes a combination of cleaner centralised energies, decentralised renewable energies and efficiency improvements, which will together provide energy services at least cost. Several such alternative studies done across the country indicate that requirement of additional capacity for power generation can be reduced by as much as 50% of that reported in the official conventional plan.

Such information could prove critical in the discourse on dams in the North-East, where states like Sikkim, Arunachal Pradesh, and Manipur keep expressing helplessness in the wake of community opposition to projects, citing the country's power requirements.

But a more fundamental concern within the region is whether these dams' juggernaut really means development for the region and whether free, prior, and informed consent of the local people has been obtained before crafting such development policies. Over the past few years, as the region has witnessed major protests over the mushrooming of several large dams, it has also had its share of supporters, not only within state governments, but also from some land owners affected by projects who look forward to financial compensation. As big business houses get ready to invest crores of rupees in these hydropower projects, sharp internal conflicts increase. Historian Arupjyoti Saikia says

> The state governments and a few others are indeed supporting these proposed investments. But the region's historical experience of exploitation of natural resources like land and oil, has led to apprehensions amongst a large section of people about the possible detrimental role of this capital—in the form of 'hydro dollars' as it has often been described by its votaries—towards the larger well being of the region. Civil society has pointed out that the colonial capital inflow into the region in the form of tea plantations could hardly generate enough economic space where the local people could have participated, besides locking off huge land resources out of their reach. The same appears to be done with the region's water. The compelling argument forwarded is that the sudden rush of capital for several mega hydropower projects is another attempt to siphon off resources from the region which itself has a small power demand. There appears to be some truth in this.

The deep involvement of youth from the North-East has been an important fact. These young people certainly want development along with economic progress. But they oppose the kind of development they feel will destroy their cultural and natural heritage. Tone Mickrow, a young leader from Arunachal Pradesh, General Secretary of the Idu Mishmi Cultural and Literary Society, the apex body of the Idu Mishmi community, says

> Can the Dibang Valley absorb this kind of mega development? We need power, but these mega dams are not the development we want. We cannot allow such massive destruction of our rivers submerging our lands, which are intricately connected with our identity. While conceiving development activities the

> absorption capacity of the region needs to be kept in mind. We would rather go in for a few micro, mini, and small hydropower projects after careful scrutiny and full public consent on a case-to-case basis. Such projects would be relatively benign. They will involve small dams on some of the tributaries, minor influx of outside labour, and will be finished in short periods. This can help us set up small scale enterprises, for example horticulture processing based ones, giving an impetus to the local economy and for providing local employment.

A banner of ACT during its June 2007–September 2009 *satyagraha* against the rush of dams in Sikkim read, 'Meaningful development, not destructive development.' But will the political economy of large dam building allow for processes to obtain the consent of local communities and debate various options for local development? The current experience is discouraging. The Idu Mishmi community has blocked the public hearing for the 3,000 MW Dibang multipurpose project no less than 10 times because they have no faith in this process as a democratic space. Their concerns appear valid as the government has already accepted ₹ 150 crore as an upfront premium from the project developers and the foundation stone for the project has been laid before completing the public consultation processes or before obtaining mandatory clearances. Despite widespread protests in Assam, no downstream public consultation has been held to date while taking decisions on upstream projects.

Where do we go from here? There are several areas which need immediate attention, but the seriousness of the situation demands that there is a moratorium on dams in the region till fundamental issues are sorted out. These include the following:

Ensuring transparency and accountability in decision-making and governance processes related to these dams at all levels—whether related to signing of MoUs, conducting impact assessment studies, or addressing transnational issues in these river basins.

Building in mechanisms to get the free, prior and informed consent of local indigenous communities.

Learning lessons from old projects in the region such as Ranganadi, Gumti, and Loktak.

Devising alternative power planning approaches at the national level and planning for assessment of genuine options and appropriate development in the ecologically and geologically fragile, seismically active, and politically and culturally sensitive river basins of the North-East.

But progress will not be possible without a widespread political debate on these issues within the region. As Akhil Gogoi of the Krishak Mukti Sangram Samiti says

> Technical issues are important. But the debate on dams in the region cannot be restricted to these issues alone. It is a matter of our rights over our natural resources. These resources are being handed over to power companies and our rivers transformed dramatically by political decisions taken in New Delhi and in the states. This requires a political response from people of the region and that will be our focus in the coming days.

(This is the abridged version of a paper published in November 2010 by Kalpavriksh, Aaranyak, and Action Aid India)

ULFA: Peace Making without Peace

Samir Kumar Das

India's north-east has been in a peace mode since the late 1990s. The incidence of insurgency and violence has reached a new low and the societies of the region, in spite of their significant variations, have been passing through a process of pacification, much of which has been militarily achieved. While pacification implies that peace is established by way of substantially weakening if not completely disarming the insurgents, peace established in this way is no recipe for enjoyment of rights, justice, and democracy. Accordingly we propose to make the finer distinction between peace and pacification. While the Naga peace process has been continuing since 1997, peace talks with the United Liberation Front of Asom (ULFA) are as old as the launch of military operations against it since the early 1990s. The mood is clearly upbeat amongst the strategists, policy makers, and perhaps civil society activists.

This chapter seeks to strike a somewhat discordant note, demystify the state of peace that has been established in Assam and is intended to (a) examine how prolonged and chronic conflicts as represented by the ULFA case acquire newer forms in course of

Unless otherwise indicated, all translations from original non-English sources are the author's.

their development; and (b) closely study the nature and quality of peace and pacification achieved in Assam and find out how older and traditional modes of managing conflicts and governing conflict resolution by the State have been rendered redundant.

Immigration, Amnesia, and Insurgency

Although ULFA was born on 7 April 1979, it was not until 1983 that it surfaced in the public arena and people became aware of its political presence in Assam.[1] The movement took a violent turn since early 1983 with inter-community clashes breaking out frequently and internal schisms cutting into the organisational strength of the All Asom Students' Union (AASU)–All Asom Gana Sangram Parishad (AAGSP) combine that led the movement. ULFA started as a more militant stream of the Assam movement and gradually broke away from the moderate forces. In 1994 I described ULFA's intervention in Assam's economic, political, and cultural life as 'decisive' (Das 1994: 51). ULFA came to limelight when it joined hands with AASU–AAGSP combine in enforcing the boycott of polls in 1983 till the names of the illegally settled 'foreigners' were struck off from the electoral rolls. The first four years of ULFA may, therefore, be regarded as the period of silent consolidation. But, as it shot into prominence by way of organising exceptionally daring bank heists, undertaking rural development works in the countryside, organising retributive killings and meting out summary justice or any of their combination. ULFA filled up the void created by the state's abdication of the responsibility of providing quick and cheap justice and development in these areas. The State, for whatever reasons, did not come down heavily on the insurgents during this period.

One wonders as to how such a State–insurgent nexus could function, particularly during the first ten years of ULFA's existence, almost without any interruption. Asom Gana Parishad (AGP) and its earlier incarnation All Assam Gana Sangram Parishad (AAGSP) and ULFA owe their common origin to the Assam movement happened between 1979 and 1985. Although organisationally and ideologically distinct, many ULFA cadres were personally close to a section of political leaders across party lines. Part of its explanation lies in the fact that ULFA enjoyed immense popularity, particularly in the late 1980s, by providing instant justice to the 'offenders' and 'criminals' and initiating rural development works. Opposition to ULFA was regarded as politically suicidal by some political parties. ULFA bore out the promise of serving as a para-state in remote areas, where the presence of the Indian State was only cosmetic. Most of the political parties were keen on deriving maximum electoral mileage from out of their presence without ever trying to crack down on them. The nexus proved to be convenient for both ULFA and other political parties till the first operation was launched against them in 1990 by the army.

By the early 1990s, in the wake of army operations, it became clear that ULFA was facing a dilemma. On the one hand, it found it difficult to operate from Assam as the heat was turned against them. On the other hand, if they were to take shelter in neighbouring Bangladesh, they would have to amend their stand on the Bangladeshi immigrants. In the latter case they would stand to lose the support of public still pitted against the 'foreigners'. One cannot say that ULFA could successfully tide over the dilemma. ULFA's survival during this period was critically dependent on its ability to inflict on the Assamese psyche the amnesia[2] of immigration, particularly from across the borders. But the memory of immigration was too horrid and vivid to be erased.

It appeared that ULFA was not opposed to a section of the immigrants, that is, those who had migrated from East Bengal. In an otherwise longish pamphlet entitled 'Asombasi Purbabangeeya Janagoshthiloi ULFAr Ahvan' (ULFA's Call to the groups from East Bengal living in Assam), ULFA redefines the concept of 'the Assamese' (*Asomiya*) as 'a people of all communities, the mixture of people who are determined to work for all-round progress of Assam'. Thus the scope of the concept no longer remained restricted only to those who speak the Assamese language as their mother tongue. Obviously, the immigrants from Bangladesh, being the largest group of immigrants, are 'an indispensable part' of them (Budhbar 1992). In an article published in the special issue of *Freedom*, ULFA's mouthpiece, to mark its 14th birth anniversary, Aniruddha Chaudhury nee Arnab Hazarika noted the great contributions made by the Bangladeshi peasants to agricultural progress.

However, there was also ambiguity in ULFA's statements. According to Sanjoy Hazarika, within one year of the publication of this pamphlet, Anup Chetiya, one of ULFA's top leaders, issued a statement which said that anyone migrating to Assam after 1971, the de facto cut-off date for the detection of foreigners agreed upon by the leaders of the Assam movement in 1985, would straightaway be branded as a 'foreigner' and most importantly as a potential deportee. A similar statement attributed to Arabinda Rajkhowa, released to the press in late 2001, reflected ULFA's continuing uneasiness with the question of foreigners.

The pamphlet on the immigrants from East Bengal, widely published in the press in Assam, contributed to its alienation from the Assamese, particularly the Assamese middle class. Udayon Misra questions:

> ... in the long run would not the ULFA's position on the infiltration issue, its clear links with Bangladesh, and its support for maximum tribal autonomy, bring into conflict with the proponents of Assamese linguistic nationalism such as the AASU and the Asom Gana Parishad? (Misra 2000: 145)

Another commentator observes, 'ULFA's pro-immigrant stand is more dictated by survival requirements rather than any ideological commitment'. ULFA found it difficult to carry the legacy of the Assam movement since the early 1990s. But the moment it started hobnobbing with Bangladesh and considered the 'people of East

Bengali origin' as an integral part of Assam it sought to distance itself from the legacy and disown it.

Organisations like AASU and regional political parties like AGP have been criticised for their obsession with the identity of the Assamese people that faces the potent threat of being swamped by the incessant immigration of people from across the borders. In fact the Assam Accord of 1985 is considered by many smaller nationalities of Assam as 'a Constitutional protective mechanism for the Assamese people – and not the people of Assam'. Bodos were the first to fall out from the larger conglomerate of the people of Assam consisting of diverse nationalities, groups, and communities that developed during the Assam movement. ULFA tried to broaden the denotation of the people of Assam by incorporating members of all communities and addressing their identity concerns.

The Vicissitudes of Peacemaking

The year 1990 was a watershed for the area, for it was in this year that the first ever military operation was conducted against ULFA. ULFA was invited by the Government of India to come and join the peace talks. In early 1990, however, ULFA looked upon any offer of negotiations as 'a clever means employed by the capitalist groups and the State of disarming ULFA' and of creating 'rift within its ranks'. ULFA's general antipathy towards dialogues is well known. Again in 1991, when the second military operation was in full swing, the government and ULFA were reportedly engaged in dialogues with the help of mediators mainly consisting of the locals from the central services and journalists.

In 1992, immediately after 'Operation Bajrang', a section of ULFA leadership was involved in peace talks, which, however, broke off when one of its delegations led by Arabinda Rajkhowa decided to withdraw due to the pressure from his uncompromising 'commander-in-chief' Paresh Barua (Misra 2000: 139). Baruah is said to have expressed his 'dissatisfaction' with the 'unconditional surrender of arms' and 'one-sided acquiescence to the Constitution of India'. Rajkhowa subsequently walked out of the talks describing his compromise-seeking colleagues as 'government revolutionaries'. Finally on 22 July 1992, a full-house general body meeting of ULFA was held at an undisclosed place in Bhutan. The meeting was attended by Arabinda Rajkhowa, Paresh Baruah, Anup Chetiya, and others. All the 18 district units, including that of Karimganj, took part in it. The meeting arrived at a 'unanimous decision' that the question of 'falling into the trap laid by the Indian State through deceit and treachery in the name of discussions does not arise' (Budhbar 29 April 1992). The meeting also decided to prepare a list of compromise-seeking leaders, describing them as 'counter-revolutionaries'. It, however, did not assign to itself the responsibility of punishing them. It resolved that the people would 'judge and punish' them.

In a signed statement issued by Mithinga Daimary, its publicity secretary, in July 1996, ULFA extended an offer of peace to the government. It set immediate stoppage of 'the forceful Indianisation of the people of Assam' as one of the preconditions. The organisation reiterated that the talks, if at all it were to be held, would centre on the issue of 'Assam's sovereignty' and it be held in 'a third country' under the UN supervision.[3] Swadhinata Phukon, one of the members of ULFA's Central Publicity Cell, pointed out that there was 'no alternative to a prolonged mass armed struggle to end killings and atrocities by the Indian State'. Again in 1999, Surrendered ULFA (SULFA) reportedly sent 'feelers' to the government circles expressing its willingness to enter into some form of peace negotiations. Immediately after the operations in Bhutan in December 2003 in which its headquarters was bust and a number of its top-ranking cadres were killed, a peace offer was made by the organisation. The issues of 'sovereignty of Assam' and 'venue of third country' for the meeting were, however, set as preconditions by Paresh Baruah, 'commander-in-chief'.

Indira Goswami, an eminent Asomiya litterateur, in her letter to the Prime Minister written in November 2004 urged the government to take steps for holding talks with the insurgents. Arabinda Rajkhowa, the outfit's chairman, also expressed his willingness to begin dialogue provided it received a formal invitation on 'the Government of India's letterhead with a signature and office seal'.

ULFA, however, seems to have moved a step forward by dropping the first two preconditions. Paresh Baruah reportedly agreed to come to New Delhi or Dispur to attend talks. He pointed out in a statement issued in August 2004, 'Sovereignty is the core issue for us and we are willing to sit for dialogue anywhere if this is discussed.'

On 19 November 2004, in one of her meetings with the Prime Minister, Indira Goswami was successful in attracting the attention of the government to the serious problem of insurgency in Assam. Goswami's move was preceded by similar moves by different organisations in the state. In September 2004, the Assam Jatiyatabadi Yuba Chhatra Parishad (AJYCP), for instance, initiated a *jatiya mahasabha* (people's council) on the dialogue process. The mahasabha called for a unilateral ceasefire by the government and asked ULFA to abjure violence. Neither of these demands was fulfilled. The AJYCP initiative was followed by several meetings organised by the intelligentsia and research organisations in Guwahati, which reiterated the demand for continuing negotiations. Notably, AASU called for a 100-hour unilateral ceasefire by the government. While the government was in no mood to concede to this demand, ULFA was critical of the presence of multiple forums outside its ambit and in a media statement in the last week of October 2004 Paresh Baruah asked these organisations to desist from such efforts.

It was in this context that an 11-member People's Consultative Group (PCG), consisting mainly of well-known civil society activists, was set up by ULFA to conduct negotiations with the government. This was the first time that ULFA inducted civil society into the peace process. It too seemed to realise the necessity of involving the larger civil society in the peace process so that the issue got widely discussed. As part of the process, Assam's collective self could be refurbished from an otherwise battered and badly fractured society. The prime minister met them in late November 2005 and the members of PCG expressed satisfaction over their first meeting with the prime minister.

Yet there were many hiccups and the initiative ended in a fiasco. First, the signals were conflicting and the government, while conducting peace talks, also continued military operations against ULFA in the Dibru–Saikhowa forests of upper Assam. In other words, the peace talks with PCG were not preceded by any suspension of operations or ceasefire agreement. There was letup in the military operations. Talks with PCG were undertaken precisely because it was not a combatant force. A ceasefire or suspension of operations can only be agreed upon by combatants. According to one estimate, while at least 13 rounds of talks were held between the Government of India and PCG, no less than 36 ULFA cadres were killed by the security forces. Moreover, the talks with PCG could not dispel the mutual hatred and suspicion between the two adversaries and clear the decks for reaching any negotiated settlement.

While ULFA stuck to its demand for release of five of its top leaders arrested in the course of the Bhutan operations in 2003 on the ground that they would take part in the peace dialogues, Tarun Gogoi, Assam's chief minister, wanted a written response from the organisation assuring of its commitment to talks. This was probably due to ULFA's record of breaking off talks after the release of their arrested leaders. The Centre, therefore, insisted on an official letter from ULFA for 'direct talks'. Gogoi went a step further and conceded that talks could be held on 'any matter' including that of 'Assam's sovereignty'. But no government on earth, he pointed out, could make the offer in black and white because of its own inherent compulsions. It may not be irrelevant to note in this connection that ULFA too insisted on written assurance from the government on the question.

The formalistic stand on both sides led to a stalemate. ULFA went on a rampage. It claimed responsibility for the carnage that killed over 70 'Hindi speakers'. These were mostly brick kiln workers from Bihar whose families, as subsequent findings indicated, had migrated to and settled in Assam more than 100 years ago. ULFA's attacks were mainly to acquire a certain visibility that it had reportedly lost as a result of the stalemate and to avenge the killing of five ULFA cadres in Kakopathar in early January by the Bihar Regiment deployed there.

It was also reported that the pressure from Inter Services Intelligence (ISI), the Pakistani espionage agency, compelled ULFA to stay away from peace talks. While direct evidence can hardly be marshalled, ULFA's refusal to enter into serious peace negotiations was regarded by many as another circumstantial evidence of being tied to a foreign intelligence agency. Indeed, Indira Goswami expressed surprise when she saw press reports that ULFA was very close to the Pakistani agency and its moves were masterminded by the latter. 'I would have given up, if only I was told', she exclaimed. Goswami, however, conceded that she did not get a specific denial when she broached the subject with ULFA chief Paresh Baruah. 'He said that they (ULFA cadres) were independent and can have ties with anybody'.

ULFA's 28th Battalion, the pro-talk group, made the offer of peace talks in 2007. The A and C Companies of the battalion under the leadership of Mrinal Hazarika, Mrinal Dutta, and Prabal Neog declared cessation of war with the security forces. The Battalion went on record saying that it did not subscribe to ULFA's demand for 'Swadhin Asom'.

> [W]e the pro-talk ULFA group looking at the (a) global political and economic situation, (b) continuous threat from the neighbouring countries surrounding Assam, (c) possible terrorist attacks in Assam by anti-Indian religious and fundamentalist groups, (d) age-old religious and cultural ties with India, have adopted a resolution in favour of Full Regional Autonomy instead of Independent Assam as a pragmatic approach (ULFA–PTF 2009: 1).

Interestingly, on 21 November 2009 Rajkhowa again reiterated ULFA's demand for 'sovereign Asom' and in a letter to the prime minister urged him to initiate peace dialogue. He wrote,

> In 2005, under your leadership and the perceived sincere efforts shown by your good self, a process for the peaceful political solution to the Indo–Asom conflict was embarked upon with high hopes. The process came unexpectedly to a halt in 2007. I am writing to you to apprise you of the decision of ULFA to restart the stalled process. I would like you to know that my organization has appointed Mr Rebati Phukon and Dr Brajen Gogoi as interlocutors between us and your government. Moreover, to take the peaceful political solution process to its decisive conclusion, i.e. restoration of sovereignty of Asom, my organization has formed a seven-member Committee comprising of (sic) 1. Bhim Kanta Burhagohain, Political Adviser; 2. Pradip Gogoi, Vice Chairman; 3. Anup Chetia, General Secretary; 4. Lieutenant-Colonel Citraban Hazarika, Finance Secretary; 5. Mr Shashadhar Choudhury, Foreign Secretary; 6. Mithinga Daimari, Publicity Secretary; 7. Mrs Pranati Hazarika, Cultural Secretary.... I trust you will receive the two interlocutors entrusted by my organization and the leaders of the same with due respect and genuine effort with total sincerity to reopen the peaceful political solution of the conflict meaningfully.[4]

The major initiative for conflict settlement was made by Assam Jatiya Mahasabha (AJM) which organised its first national convention on 24 April 2010. More than 109 organisations, activists, and intellectuals from across the state gathered in Guwahati to chalk out the modalities of possible talks between Government of India and ULFA. The draft resolution of the convention made a plea to the top leaders of both the government and ULFA for sitting together to resolve all issues.

'All core issues of the ULFA, including the issue of sovereignty, can be discussed. However, both the government and the ULFA should shun violence.'

On the occasion of ULFA's 32nd anniversary in April 2011, Arabinda Rajkhowa, its chairman and one of the leading minds involved in talks with the government, in his address to the people of Assam redefined the colonial character of Assam. He welcomed the 'promise' of a 'respectable and acceptable solution' that he claims to have received from the Government of India. He argued,

> Although the United Liberation Front of Assam harbours an armed resistance programme in Assam, it wants a peaceful political solution to the Indo–Assam conflict. Any military solution to the conflict is a position opposed to ULFA's principles and Constitution (Sanjukta Mukti Bahini 2011: 24).

While strongly disputing that they have relinquished their demand for 'Swadhin Assam', he highlights the importance of discussions and conventions in order to find out a 'durable solution to the question of Assam's existence' (Sanjukta Mukti Bahini 2011: 18).

While by all accounts, 'sovereignty of Assam' is no longer considered an option by the pro-talks leadership, ULFA emphasised the need for exploring the option of 'full autonomy' to be obtained from within the purview of the Constitution of India. Pradip Gogoi, ULFA's vice chairman, elaborated the idea in an interview, 'We want utmost stress on the true federal structure of the Constitution. This has to be worked out. Ethnic reconciliation is needed in Assam and that can be ensured only through genuine Constitutional mechanism' (Deb 2011: 19).

The demand for 'full autonomy' was being raised by the pro-talks group of ULFA for some time. The group, while addressing an audience comprising academics, students, journalists, public intellectuals, voluntary workers, and writers in Guwahati in July 2009, expressed its desire to interact with the general public (it was cut off from the general public after the organisation was banned and its leaders and cadres were on the run) and declared,

> Our duty is to build up a favourable environment and public opinion for a talk between the Government and the Central Committee of ULFA. From Sadiya to Dhuburi (sic) we will build up public opinion for the talk. We will be the catalyst between the Government of India and ULFA.[5]

It seems that ULFA approached the National Convention for guidance and advice but asserted its autonomous identity by continuing to insist on its demand for 'sovereign Asom'. It is, for instance, argued that ULFA did not seek such guidance and advice when it decided to take up arms. Hence, according to Sabhapandit, ULFA was free to take whatever decision it could without seeking the guidance and advice from the National Convention (Sabhapandit 2011: 13). But if it were to be in the 'national interest' (meaning in the interest of Assam and the Assamese), then the guidance and advice from the National Convention are more than necessary.

What if the talks failed? ULFA was desperate to initiate talks as well as in ensuring that those did not fail. More than the government, it was now the pro-talk groups of ULFA that wanted to enter into talks. In 2009, Jiten Dutta, one of ULFA's top ranking leaders, had argued,

> We will not say now what we will do but we will take some decisive steps. The government has turned a deaf ear towards the issue. Despite repeated requests to clear its stand, there is simply no response from the government. This will be our final meeting with the government as we want to clear the air once and for all (Barman 2009: 110).

While the above statement sought to retain the right to go back to the jungles and take up arms if the demand was not met, ULFA too realised that the cost of going back to the jungles might be too high compared to the cost involved in failed peace talks. The question in the post-pacification campaign was not how much was gained. The question was how much one could do to minimise the comparative costs by way of making a choice for the least damaging option.

On 3 September 2011 as the first step towards ushering in permanent peace in Assam, a tripartite agreement for Suspension of Operations (SoO) was signed between the Central government, the Assam government and ULFA. The Union government was represented by the Joint Secretary (North-East), Ministry of Home Affairs, and the Assam government by the Home Commissioner. Shahdhar Chaudhuri, Chitraban Hazarika, and Raju Barua, three key functionaries represented ULFA.

ULFA pro-talk faction (ULFA-PTF) sought an amendment in the Constitution of India for finding 'meaningful' ways to protect the rights and identity of indigenous people of Assam dropping its earlier demand for Sovereignty. In the 'charter of demands' submitted to Home Minister P. Chidambaram, Arabinda Rajkhowa, chairman of ULFA-PTF, said, 'We demand constitutional and political arrangements and reforms, including protection of the identity and material resources of indigenous population of Assam'. On the issue of Paresh Baruah's (ULFA anti-talk faction – ULFA-ATF) opposition to any dialogue with the government if 'sovereignty' issue was not on the table, ULFA-PTF 'Foreign Secretary' Shashadhar Choudhury said, 'Baruah himself is yet to make any comment about the peace process. We hope that one day he will join in the talks'. He added that of late there had been no contact with Baruah and he was 'probably' living in Myanmar.[6]

Conclusions

While insurgency and violence are only more congealed forms of conflict along a scale, these acquire certain momentum in the sense that the causes that have inspired them are gradually being pushed into the background without resolving. In an essay written in 2005, I have shown how conflict existed everywhere in the North-East as a 'complex cacophony' of voices and how all these voices become articulated into a mega-conflict rendering many a voice hitherto involved in the cacophony redundant. Prolonged violence and insurgency are seen to requisition newer 'causes' in order to sustain themselves or these are simply 'forgotten' and dried up. Sanjib Baruah designates the process as the 'disappearance of conflicts'. Many of the conflicts in history are not resolved; they simply 'disappear', thanks to their chronic and prolonged character. The ULFA case points out how the way one seeks to solve a given conflict catalyses into another series of conflicts. Originated as a conflict between what Prafulla Mahanta calls 'citizens' and 'foreigners', Assam brings to our attention an entire morphology of conflicts. It shows how what began with the threefold demand for detection, disenfranchisement, and deportation of 'foreigners' eventually mutated into a demand for 'sovereign Assam'. The upshot of pacification carried out for over the last two decades is that ULFA, or at least a section of it, realises that the cost of fighting from the jungles is not only un-affordably high but will not attain the objective. In fact isolation from Assam and her people alienates it. With it comes the realisation that peace cannot be achieved by sticking to what one sets forth as one's objectives but by listening to others, other stakeholders, the SJA in particular. Peace emerges out of a complicated process of dialogue.

Now that the nature of conflict has transformed beyond recognition and it is not the same conflict that gets addressed, peace-making too has acquired newer forms. In the first phase of insurgency, state measures consisted of (a) counter-insurgency operations; (b) conceding to the demands of insurgents by way of establishing some form of a homeland (statehood within the Indian Union, ADC, recognition of traditional institutions, etc); and (c) development by creating dependency through grant of doles and subsistence.

Tripura is no exception to this trend. It is now being increasingly realised that each of these measures has its snowballing effect on violence and insurgency in the region. While peace accords set off ethnic consolidation and homogenisation, the democratic agenda of justice highlights the necessity of reconciliation by way of recognising difference. The post-accord society in Mizoram is often identified as 'Mizo society' and self-determination claims of other non-Mizo communities refuse to subscribe to such a simple identification. Much in the same manner the second generation problems of insurgency led by ULFA have already cropped up. None of the Bodo organisations forms part of SJA fearing that 'sovereign Assam' might not necessarily imply autonomy for the Bodos let alone 'sovereign Bodoland'.

ULFA will listen to voices of others as much as to reorient its demands to be negotiated during peace talks. The government also knows that it is not dealing with the same demand for 'sovereign Assam' and that they will not return to the jungles. It is a new post-conflict Assam that refuses to understand the language of violence. The government will wait for the transformation of the demand for 'sovereign Assam' into a 'developed Assam' with its vision enshrined in LEP documents and Vision 2020. The old technologies of addressing conflicts will not work but will the balm of development work? Only the future will bear out.

Notes

1. This is only a brief summary of an otherwise detailed history of ULFA from 1979 to 1991. (See Das 1994: 68–89).
2. Veena Das has analysed the role of amnesia in sparking off the Khalistan movement.
3. ULFA has more or less stuck to these three preconditions since 1992 until recently.
4. Letter to the prime minister.
5. Translated from the original Assamese by Prateeti Barman
6. http://www.satp.org/satporgtp/countries/india/states/assam/terrorist_outfits/ULFA_tl.htm accessed on 2 January 2012.

References

Sanjukta Mukti Bahini. 2011. 'Asomar Dwi-Trinshatitam Pratishtha Diwas Upalakshe Sabhapati Arabinda Rajkhowar Abhibhasanar Sampadit Rupar Kiyadansha' (in Assamese) [United Liberation Front of Assam, Excerpts from the edited version of the address of President Arabinda Rajkhowa on the occasion of the thirty-second birth anniversary], *Pahekiya Aami* 6(2), 15–30 April.

Barman, Prateeti. 2009. *Changing Perception of Freedom: Civil Society and Its Response to United Liberation Front of Asom*. New Delhi: Akansha.

Das, Samir Kumar. 1994. *ULFA: A Political Analysis,* Delhi: Ajanta.

Deb, Swati. 2011. 'ULFA Peace Talks: All that Glitters Might not be Gold'. *Eastern Panorama* XIX(3), March.

Misra, Udayon. 2000. *The Periphery Strikes Back: Challenges to the Nation-State in Assam and Nagaland.* Shimla: Indian Institute of Advanced Study.

Sabhapandit, Ranjit. 2011. 'Purna swattasasan, ULFA-sarkarar alochana: Asombasiye ki bishayak loi alochana bichare' (in Assamese). [Full autonomy, talks between ULFA and government: What the people of Assam want to discuss], *Prantik* 30(13), 1 June.

ULFA-PTF. 2009. 'Charter of Demands to the Prime Minister of India'. Pro-Talk Faction, 28th Battalion, February.

Corruption and Insurgency in the North-East

E.N. Rammohan

The British East India Company (EIC) ruled Assam and the hill states of the north-east. Control of Manipur and Tripura was indirect as they were princely states. They began their rule in early 19th century after defeating the invading Burmese forces from Upper Assam and Manipur. They found that tea grows well in Assam. Subsequently they established tea gardens as also their administration over Assam and Manipur. They found that there was no trading community in these places. The two states had a barter economy. The EIC had come for trading. They, therefore, brought the Marwari community from Calcutta where they had already been established. In Manipur, the Marwaris established themselves in Imphal and took over the trade in rice and other commodities. In Assam, they opened shops in the tea gardens and major towns. In a sense, we can say that this also saw the institution of corruption in the North-East.

The first agitation caused by corruption was the 'Nupi Lan' movement in Manipur. This agitation was led by women Meithei traders in Imphal against the Marwari traders for hoarding and diverting rice outside Manipur when there was a shortage in the state.

In 1859, the British government took over control from EIC and ruled this area directly except for the princely states of Manipur and

Tripura. Corruption existed in the states directly ruled by the British but mainly among the petty bureaucracy. In Manipur the Raja's rule was not as clean as the directly ruled states. Tripura was better. In 1949, Government of India took over Manipur by forcing the Raja to sign an instrument of accession. The Central government then declared Manipur as a Union Territory and very soon a number of unfeeling bureaucrats took over the administration from the Raja and corruption took a quantum leap in Manipur.

The situation became really exacerbated when the Naga Hills District was given statehood in 1963 after the Nagas had been waging a bush war since 1955. The Central government had earlier managed to win over a section of the Naga National Council (NNC). The government granted generous funds to the new state. With it, they also sent a group of unholy contractors to the North-East who managed to corner all the contracts for supply of stores to the new state. By now the headquarters of all the main Central government departments had come up in Shillong. The HQ of the old North East Frontier Agency (NEFA) had also been located in Shillong. The Congress party was in power in Delhi as also in some of the north-eastern states. Very soon the contractors who came from Delhi earned the dubious nomenclature of 'Delhi Durbar'. This was in reference to their favoured status in getting all the supply contracts for the north-eastern states. They also established their HQ in Shillong.

The method of looting the state was simple and direct. Any commodity being supplied, be it CGI sheets, bricks, cement, medicines, hospital equipment, civil supplies like rice or sugar, those were always over-invoiced. If 100 quantity of an item was supplied, the bill was invariably for 1000 quantity and the charge taken report would naturally show 1000 quantity. This was a standard method. If a 100 km road was to be built, the materials would be shown supplied for 1000 km. Very often no road would be built at all. But it would be shown as built in the books. In all the hill areas of the north-east hundreds of roads have been built on paper.

I worked for a short time as the Superintendent of Police of the Central Bureau of Investigation (CBI) in Shillong, looking after all the states of the north-east, except Tripura. It was child's play to detect cases of corruption and register cases in the Shillong branch of the CBI from all the six states. However, it was extremely difficult to get the cases charge-sheeted. If the contractor was a member of the 'Delhi Durbar', it was hundred per cent certain that the case would be closed on orders from CBI HQ. When Emergency was declared in 1975, the CBI became a handmaiden of the party in power!

It is a natural corollary that the extraordinary amount of corruption fuelled insurgencies all over the north-east. The immediate cause of insurgency in any one of these states may have been different, but its continuation was invariably initiated by this fact.

The Naga insurgency started because many of the Naga people felt that they were culturally, socially, and genetically different from people of mainland India. They felt that they would not be comfortable under the laws framed for India in general. This was true to a very large extent. However, the leaders of the tribal people in all the hill states adapted very well indeed to the culture of corruption. The indigenous political parties operating in these states as also the national parties were equally adept at swiping money from any project set up for the North-East. It was also interesting to see how some of the regional parties adapted to this almost umbilical link with the party in power in Delhi! If the Congress lost and another party formed the government in Delhi, the ruling party in some of the north-eastern states immediately switched en bloc to the new party!

I was Advisor to the Governor of Manipur in 2002. When it was known that elections were going to be declared soon, some regional party MLAs asked me whether the Congress party was likely to win. I told them that that was immaterial. If the AIDMK, a Tamil Nadu regional party, would come to power, all of them would join this party, without even knowing what AIDMK stood for! They were not ashamed at all at my contemptuous remark, but asked me what AIDMK stood for! I did not enlighten them.

Manipur leads the race for the first prize in the scale of corruption. The state has accordingly the largest number of militant groups. While the hard core People's Liberation Army (PLA) and the United National Liberation Front (UNLF) have remained intact, most of the other insurgent groups have split into so many factions that it is difficult to keep pace with them.

However, some of the biggest scams have occurred in Assam. One was in the veterinary department at Demow, a small town in Sibsagar sub-division. The scam was started during the Assam Gana Parishad (AGP) period during 1985–90. Fake letters of credit (LOCs) were sent to the Demow veterinary office and fake bills were passed by them. The fake LOCs were in lakhs of rupees. It surprised me when it was finally detected. How was this scam not detected earlier? Copies of LOCs go to the Sub-Divisional Officer (SDO), the Treasury Officer, and the State Bank of India (SBI) manager. Besides, reconciliation is done from time to time by the Accountant General. Obviously, no one had touched it in the state government as political leaders were involved! The most interesting fact was that when the AGP government was replaced by the Congress in the next election, there was a handing/taking over of the scam! It was an alert young Deputy Commissioner of Sibsagar who detected this and reported it to the Chief Secretary. It is also to the credit of the Additional Chief Secretary, that he enquired into the case and revealed the whole scam. Ultimately, the CBI took over the investigation but the case was closed as one accused died. There were all kinds of rumours as to how another accused got round the CBI in closing the case!

This scam had nothing to do with insurgency. It neither spawned an insurgency nor did it indirectly start one. However, one fact is certain, which is that the continued siphoning off of funds from the north-eastern states has indirectly spawned insurgencies in Nagaland, Manipur, Meghalaya, Garo Hills, and the North Cachar Hills.

One of the biggest scams that continues forever in the North-East is the diversion of civil supplies items from the railheads. Regularly rice, wheat, and sugar are downloaded at the rail heads in Dimapur, Tinsukhia, New Guwahati, and Bongaigaon. These are diverted to the black market. To add insult to injury, fake transport bills for the items diverted are claimed from the capitals at Kohima, Imphal etc. This is how the PLA landed at the SBI in Imphal when five transport contractors were about to cash their bills for fake transportation. The insurgents asked the contractors to sign the receipts for the amounts and then took the cash and disappeared! They told them that as they had not transported the goods, they had no right to the money!

AFSPA: A Contentious Instrument in a Democratic Polity

Patricia Mukhim

The Armed Forces (Special Powers) Act (AFSPA) was passed in 1958 by the Indian Parliament to quell the rebellion in the so-called 'disturbed areas' in the states of Arunachal Pradesh, Assam, Manipur, Meghalaya, Mizoram, Nagaland and Tripura. It was later extended to Jammu and Kashmir and named it the Armed Forces (Jammu and Kashmir) Special Powers Act, 1990 and was invoked in July 1990. This Act is a legacy of a colonial power. The Armed Forces (Special Powers) Ordinance, 1942, was used by the British to quell dissent during the Second World War. In a way it is a reincarnation of the Rowlatt Act which allowed the British to imprison any Indian suspected to be involved in terrorist activities. The protest against this Act led to the Jallianwala Bagh massacre which is one of the greatest blots on British imperialism. Like the Rowlatt Act which the British clearly stated was to be used in emergency situations, the AFSPA too was intended for the same purpose. So would it be fair to say that India's North-East has been in an emergency situation since 1958 and Jammu and Kashmir since 1990? Or better still, is this an implicit statement that the Indian State is waging a war against its own people and using all forms of brutality to secure the nation-building agenda of the State?

According to AFSPA, in an area that is proclaimed as 'disturbed', an officer of the armed forces has the following powers.

- After giving such due warning, fire upon or use other kinds of force even if it causes death, against the person who is acting against law or order in the disturbed area for the maintenance of public order.
- Destroy any arms dump, hide-outs, prepared or fortified position or shelter or training camp from which armed attacks are made by the armed volunteers or armed gangs or absconders wanted for any offence.
- Arrest without a warrant anyone who has committed cognizable offences or is reasonably suspected of having done so and may use force if needed for the arrest.
- Enter and search any premise in order to make such arrests, or to recover any person wrongfully restrained or any arms, ammunition or explosive substances and seize it.
- Stop and search any vehicle or vessel reasonably suspected to be carrying such person or weapons.
- Any person arrested and taken into custody under this Act shall be made over to the officer in charge of the nearest police station with the least possible delay, together with a report of the circumstances occasioning the arrest.
- Army officers have legal immunity for their actions. There can be no prosecution, suit or any other legal proceeding against anyone acting under that law. Nor is the government's judgment on why an area is found to be disturbed subject to judicial review.
- Protection of persons acting in good faith under this Act from prosecution, suit or other legal proceedings, except with the sanction of the Central Government, in exercise of the powers conferred by this Act.

For declaring an area as 'disturbed' there must be a grave situation of law and order on the basis of which the governor or administrator can form opinion that an area is in such a disturbed or dangerous condition that use of armed forces is necessary to assist civil administration. In Jammu and Kashmir the Act has been enforced since 1990. It was repealed in some constituencies of Manipur in August 2004.

Needless to say this Act has been followed more in the breach than compliance. The first clause authorising army to fire on a suspect even to the point of causing death after giving sufficient warning is a licence to eliminate anyone 'suspected' to be a terrorist. The state has used this Act to justify its actions of killing those it 'suspected' were aiding and abetting terrorists. In a close knit society everybody, including the militants, insurgents, or terrorists (depending on how they are labelled), have families, friends, and even sympathisers whom they visit on and off. Can everyone be called a suspect? What is interpreted as 'collusion' by the Indian state is actually a 'caring concern' by family and friends who wish to reach out to their 'misguided' son, brother, or husband, very often to tell them to give up the armed struggle because it yields nothing but death. To believe that entire families and societies support militancy is an over-statement. For the army to consider an entire community as colluding against the state and to unleash AFSPA on them is an act of grave violation of human rights on an entire region where the Act operates. And the fear that the army and para-military forces like AR, which is trained and led by the army, needs to be on constant standby and the Act cannot be revoked defies the very notion of justice. This also shows the Indian state as a brutal force juxtaposed against a population it considers renegade. That we from the region have remained silent over the continued use of AFSPA and have allowed a lone woman, Irom Sharmila, to carry this huge burden on her frail shoulders is also a commentary of how we have been pushed into a corner. The people of the eight states elected 26 Members of Parliament (MPs) to represent their aspirations in the highest edifice of democracy, the Lok Sabha. But till date the MPs have not made a strong pitch for the revocation of AFSPA in the region. Civil society from the entire region too have not attempted to network among themselves or with the larger Indian civil society or with the people of Jammu and Kashmir to make a common cause on the issue.

However, there are other issues that need our attention and where we need to apply our collective thoughts and wisdom. While we all make a hue and cry on removing AFSPA many of us gloss over the fact that the Disturbed Areas Act (DAA) precedes the invocation of AFSPA. The former is a state law and can be revoked by the state government. AFSPA thereafter becomes redundant because you cannot have extraordinary measures being invoked if the situation does not warrant it. However, Colonel Sanjay Viswas Rao, 15 Corps, Srinagar, maintained that DAA has no relation with AFSPA. He said that it was a misconception that the two laws are linked to each other. He further said Kashmir was classified as a 'disturbed' area by a Parliament resolution, making it possible to apply AFSPA in J&K. In other states, however, DAA is a state law which gives extraordinary powers to police in a 'disturbed' area. According to Rao, DAA was supposed to be extended every year but last time it was extended in 1997. DAA thus does not even exist in J&K today but AFSPA continues to function. These dichotomies need to be paid attention to and discussed and debated.

Interestingly, what Rao says goes counter to what Union Home Minister P. Chidambaram and several other politicians and legal experts have stated. They said that the state government can make AFSPA non-applicable by revoking DAA. So where do we stand? Who is correct? The army and by extension the Defence Ministry or the Union Home Ministry?

In December last year the Manipur government decided to extend DAA for one more year. This automatically activates AFSPA. The reason given by Ibobi Singh, Chief Minister of Manipur, for extension of DAA is the burgeoning armed movement. The cabinet decided to extend DAA based on reports from security agencies—army, police, and para-military forces—in the state. Are these the only correct sources? In a democracy, where does the voice of the people stand? Has there been an audit carried out of the ground situation? Is there a vested interest for the army and the huge contingent of para-military forces to park themselves in Manipur? Has there ever been a dispassionate study of the impact of long periods of militarisation on the psyche of the people of Manipur? Has the state not further alienated the people of this region by treating them as 'potential agent provocateurs' for decades? When Gen V.K. Singh took over as the army chief he was asked if there would be army operations in the Maoist hit areas. His immediate response was that the army cannot be used to fight its own people. Why is the army being used indiscriminately to fight its own people in north-east India and J&K? What is the answer of the Defence Ministry and the central government to this ambivalence?

AFSPA has often been considered and used as the only instrument to deal with insurgency. More effective policing measures have not been at all explored to the full. The Act was invoked in Assam excluding North Cachar Hills District and the areas already notified as 'disturbed areas' under Section 3 of the Assam Disturbed Areas Act, 1955 (Act No. XIX of 1955) and under Section 3 of the Armed Forces (Special Powers) Act, 1958 and No. PLB. 25/80/11, both dated 27 February 1980. But the operation of the two notifications was stayed by a court order on a petition filed by a citizen on 7 April 1980. The state of Assam and the Union of India filed a Special Leave Petition (Civil) No. 4377 of 1980 before the Supreme Court of India which ordered the Gauhati High Court to dispose of the stay application after hearing both sides on 18 April 1980. The Supreme Court ruled that the application of DAA and AFSPA are within the purview of the Constitution.

But can AFSPA be applied in areas where the state is already in talks with the militants/insurgents or where it can be stated that there has been no public disorder so as to warrant extraordinary measures? This is true of Nagaland where NSCN (Isak Muivah - IM) has been engaged in peace talks with the government since 1997. In Assam most of the ethnic militant groups, such as National Democratic Front of Bodoland (NDFB), Dima Hasao Daoga (DHD), Kuki Longri National Front (KLNF) etc. have expressed their keenness to come to the table for talks. Even ULFA, one of the most virulent militant groups in Assam the Chairman of which had come over-ground, is now ready for talks. Casualties on account of militancy are on the wane. To continue with AFSPA in such a situation is to lend credence to the allegations that it is a police state where all constitutional rights and liberties have been suspended. Tripura is touted as the state where militancy was brought down by the police and not by the use of the military. Even here AFSPA continues to be used in the tribal inhabited areas. That no one has questioned the Manik Sarkar government on this issue is surprising. It also shows that each state in the region has been insulated from each other although all suffer from the same predicament. The tribal voice in Tripura is so weak that they are in no position to demand the repeal of AFSPA or DAA. Both these Acts have been kept dangling like the sword of Damocles over the tribals of Tripura to be unleashed in case of any outbreak of trouble. The Government of Tripura repeatedly claims that it has brought down insurgency. Then why the continued imposition of the Act?

It is, therefore, a great opportunity for all the seven states to make a common cause on AFSPA and to push the Government of India to take a call on whether it is good for the policy to continue and to look at the North-East purely from the prism of a security zone. How long will it take for people here to prove their good conduct? The Indian State must understand the genesis of violence here as well as what spurs it. It must address the root causes rather than using extraordinary measures to quell violence without having adequately understood the larger aspirations of the people.

Impunity, Vulnerability, and AFSPA

Sanjoy Hazarika

Over the past decades, my colleagues and I have met many people whose lives had been changed irrevocably by the decades of violence that had gripped the north-eastern states of India. Particularly in Nagaland, Assam, Tripura, Manipur, and Mizoram, villagers have borne the brunt of contesting ideas and forces. Many families and individuals tell stories of personal loss, bereavement, and physical and emotional trauma. For many of them, those campaigning for rights, people from media or academics, and researchers were often the first point of interaction with people from another part of India, who sat among and listened to them. These are stories that the world does not know of, or has not cared to know, thus indirectly contributing to silencing the voices from the margins. We believe that telling these stories would act as a form of political intervention and empowerment building bridges between communities and helping to open up a little known region and an alienated people to public consciousness.

Analysts say war and conflict are devastating to social and cultural institutions because they impact societies and individuals. Every person who has survived conflict is in some way scarred by her or his experience. It takes people and society a long time to come to terms with what happened.

A young woman in Dimapur shared her experience. She is a member of a women's association which works like an informal, tribal panchayat which handles social cases of women. Her village, she said, was bombed by the Indian Air Force in the 1960s. She was only a baby at that time. Her mother, while running away from the burning village, hid her in the hollow of a tree thinking she would come back and retrieve her when it was safe. It was three days before she could come back. The child lay inside that hollow hungry, frightened, and alone.

We wondered, 'What must she have been thinking during that time? What impact would this have left on her?'

The trauma haunted her, she said. As soon as she was old enough she went to join her father, who was a member of the Naga army fighting the Indian State. It was only much later that she came to terms with what had happened to her village, to herself and her father, who was killed in the course of battles with the army. She learnt forgiveness and turned to the Church, which is a very powerful institution in Nagaland and other parts of the North-East.

It is obvious that women have faced violence in situations of conflict. What this means in terms of the impacts is still being studied. The most obvious impact is physical and/or sexual violence. However, the psychological scarring as a result of prolonged exposure to brutality has an even deeper impact on their lives. Women experience violence from three fronts: the State, the militants, and a corresponding escalation of domestic violence. The effects of violent acts like rape, sexual abuse, and assault lead to emotional trauma, what is known as post-traumatic stress disorder. Again, this is something that is being understood only now. Facilities like trauma and counseling centres in such cases are few and totally inadequate to deal with the complexity and scale of the problem.

Dr P. Ngully is a psychiatrist from Nagaland and was associated with a study I had helped conduct (Bearing Witness: the Impact of Conflict on Women in Nagaland and Assam, 2011, in collaboration with the Heinrich Boll Foundation). He is among the very few specialists who have looked at this problem in Nagaland. Nagaland has faced confrontation and violence both from the State and non-State groups for over 50 years. The sight of a uniformed person evokes fear and terror in villagers in Nagaland. 'They have rarely seen any other face of India barring the army and the paramilitary, which they associate with harassment and violent behaviour', according to Dr Ngully.

In fact, respondents to the survey and interviews set out therein were posited on a set of questions developed by the National Institutes of Health (US) (NIH) and internationally accepted, as indicative of whether a person has suffered or is suffering from post-traumatic stress disorder (PTSD). This questionnaire was prepared as a prerequisite to the identification of the 'victims' to be interviewed under the project. This was done on the advice of two prominent psychiatrists. These were the hinges which opened the doors to an unprecedented and moving outpouring of experiences, narrations and stories from victims. The questions were the following:

'In your life did you ever had so frightening, horrible or upsetting experience that, in the past month

1. Did you have had nightmares about it or thought about it when you did not want to?
2. Did you try hard not to think about it or went out of your way to avoid situations that reminded you of it?
3. Were you constantly on guard, watchful, or easily startled?
4. Did you feel numb or detached from others, from activities, or your own surroundings?'

This approach helped women to share their experiences of coping with the realities of daily life, experiences which they perhaps would not have felt confident enough to share where it not for the fact that the research teams in both states chosen for the study were 'local' and that contacts with those interviewed were made with extensive help from friends, neighbours, civil society groups, local women's groups, local interpreters, and guides.

Women, after all, are responsible in these situations as mothers of children, and wives of the wounded. They are innocent victims of wars and conflicts not of their making. They suffer as civilians with greater restrictions placed on them. They are assaulted, raped, humiliated, beaten, and murdered during conflicts. They are displaced, turned out of their homes, disinherited, widowed, or orphaned. They lose their children to bullets and violence. Many just disappear without a trace. Others are trafficked across state and national borders and face a nightmarish life of sexual abuse and disease.

The loss that they face is not just emotional or physical but transfers into the economic and social spheres as well. Most women face a decline in social legitimacy and find themselves relegated to the fringes of society with no one to care for them or to speak on their behalf.

They form the bulk of the unemployed and the uneducated. They, therefore, find themselves unable and ill-equipped to take on the burden of the household. As a result they become completely poverty stricken. Young widows are forced to head households, even though in a patriarchal feudal setup they have little or no access to land and property. In tribal societies the economic burden is generally considered the primary responsibility of women and for this reason perhaps they get very little help from men or from the State in the aftermath of violence when the work of reconstruction begins. In Nagaland, for example, women do extensive fieldwork as in so many hill communities. In addition, they carry on with 'normal' life and do 'normal' chores such as cooking, washing, fetching water, and bringing up and nurturing children to sustain their households.

Other impacts of conflict include loss of livelihoods and food scarcity due to destruction of fields and farmlands, basic infrastructure like roads and bridges, hospitals, shelters, and schools. Women are forced to take on the role of food providers and caretakers of the old, infirm, wounded, and young. In times of war women's access to public spaces becomes even more restricted and their mobility further hampered because of the presence of security forces and armed militia. All too often their bodies become objects of battle with both sides treating them as the spoils of war. Women who lose their 'honour' find it extremely difficult to lead normal lives as well as to live down the stigma. There is total breakdown of structures, norms of behaviour, and socially sanctioned behaviour. The result is atrocities and human rights abuses reported by print, visual, and audio media.

When there is a complete turnaround of the known circumstances, the familiar life and exchanging it for the unfamiliar, the uncertain, the insecure, and the dangerous, how do people, especially women, who are the most vulnerable sections of the society, cope with it? What happens when they are forced to flee, to leave the familiar environments of their villages and towns, and find themselves cut off from their tribes and cultural moorings? What dangers confront them in their new environments? These are difficult and challenging issues and troubling questions.

Continued violence, especially in the rural areas, has resulted in large scale migration of young women and men to urban centres. Without any effective support system, they become extremely vulnerable to exploitation, violence, and trafficking. The incidence of HIV/AIDS, drug abuse, alcohol and substance abuse increases substantially in such situations. The feminisation of the AIDS epidemic is becoming all too apparent and the increased vulnerability of women to HIV/AIDS in situations of conflict is an area of growing concern to social and health activists. The presence of large number of armed forces also increases the demand for sex workers. Young women get sucked into the situation and become pawns in a larger brutal network that thrives on human misery and conflict. Human and drug trafficking proliferate with women and children being sent to other parts of the country. This also results from the loss of other economic options and increased poverty as a result of longstanding conflict situations.

The state of women's health is another picture of neglect and apathy in areas of conflict. There is lack of infrastructure, adequate facilities, and health personnel. Most of the central government's much hyped health schemes remain on paper with few able to access these. Travels to the remote hinterland of both Nagaland and Assam revealed to us how the most marginalised segments of its population hardly figure in the 'Incredible India' campaign promoted by large corporations and governments, marching, the public is informed, towards 'development' and 'health for all'.

Another important point to note here is as to what is happening to the young people, 'the children of the conflict', who increasingly leave their violent homelands for education and jobs elsewhere in the country? There are large numbers of students who flock Delhi University every year. A Manipuri professor in Delhi says that there is a Manipuri student in every house in a colony behind the capital's Patel Chest Institute. There has been a social impact of this out-migration. Even vegetable sellers there have picked up the Meitei language. While this is significant, we must also look at the other side of the social dimensions of this migration. What does the movement of a large amount of human resource capital mean for a small conflict-ridden state? Do these youth ever go back and if so to what?

By conducting interviews, travelling with research teams into remote villages and engaging in conversations with victims of conflicts, we have come across several striking stories and experiences.

It is important to consider how the Armed Forces (Special Powers) Act (AFSPA) discriminates among citizens, creating specially privileged individuals and groups who function with both impunity and immunity, i.e. they are literally above the law which applies only for 'others'.

Enacted in 1958 to deal with the Naga uprising in the then composite state of Assam, AFSPA was reviewed by the Justice B.P.

Jeevan Reddy Committee in 2005, which recommended that it be scrapped.

The Reddy Committee report has not been tabled in Parliament, despite the recent outcry triggered by the Justice Verma Committee's view that the Act needs to be reviewed (in the light of sexual offences committed by men in uniform). Three reviews, including the Reddy Committee, recommended the repeal of the Act. AFSPA contains mainly six clauses. The critical ones permit security forces to open fire and even kill upon suspicion. Criminal prosecution of soldiers involved in such acts will need the Centre's sanction. New Delhi has not given even a single sanction in over half a century.

In my view, it creates four degrees of difference, of separation, among all Indians, enshrining discrimination into law and the system.

First, it creates a category which is above the law and thus protected by AFSPA, providing nothing short of absolute immunity to them. These are members of the security forces who are covered by the Act.

The second category comprises of those who are vulnerable to the Act because they are unprotected by it and are at the mercy of security forces. Ironically because of the brutality of the experience of this law, ordinary people lump with those who are truly anti-State such as insurgents, militants, and armed groups. These organisations and their members are supposed to be the principal targets of such a law. They are by no measure innocents or part of the general category of citizenship.

The third group comprises of those who are unaffected by the Act, for example those living in other parts of the country where it is not in use. The Act is used in border belts of Arunachal Pradesh and Meghalaya as well as in Tripura though none of these states have a 'live' insurgency. One of the reasons why the Marxists roared their way back to power in Tripura was surely because they had resolved the insurgency situation. It is a blessing that a huge majority of the population of India is untouched by it although Punjab had a sharp and brutal tryst with it during the pro-separatist movement during the 1980s and 1990s before the police and local politicians moved to take charge of the situation, sending the army back to barracks where it belongs in, what Finance Minister P. Chidambaram has defined as, a civilian government.

There is a fourth category of citizens, which is increasingly becoming a reality in the states where AFSPA is in place, anchoring its arbitrariness and anti-democratic core. The police forces, especially those in Manipur (where police commandos strike as much fear as the armed forces), behave as if they are protected by the law and enjoy immunity under it. Indeed, if there is one good reason why AFSPA should be repealed, apart from all the reasons cited by human rights campaigners, it is the resultant atmosphere of immeasurable impunity which comes with a sense of immunity that has transcended the law and infected the 'civilian' administration.

The human rights activists' campaign against AFSPA has been built around questioning the right and capacity of soldiers to shoot and kill suspects without being prosecuted in a civilian court of law. Over 55 years of use and misuse of the Act in the North-East has bred such a climate of impunity that law enforcers have become the primary law breakers. That climate of impunity appears to have infected the political and administrative structure in the states. The recent arrest of the scion of a powerful Manipuri politician in a case where an army colonel had been arrested with a huge consignment of drugs headed for Myanmar underscores the social and political disaster overwhelming the region. The money trail leads to new oligarchies, created by the protective presence of this monstrous law.

While the Supreme Court said in 1997 that the law was Constitutional and as per due process (Justice J.S. Verma, whose Committee has drawn such support on issues of sexual assault, was the Chief Justice at that time), it does not mean that the 'justness' of the law was upheld. A law can be Constitutional but it can also be unjust. One is a moral dimension, the other is a technicality. That is the case with AFSPA.

The current Law Minister Ashwani Kumar has erred by defending the Centre's decision not to move sexual assault and rape out of the purview of protection of AFSPA. In an interview, he said that AFSPA applied in 'conflict zones and difficult circumstances where the onus and burden of proof was not easy to resolve; therefore, the opinion of the defence establishment and intelligence agencies was critical in such matters'. Is the Government of India saying that it is necessary to protect specific acts of omission and commission by its armed forces because it cannot trust civilian process? The Air Force correctly sends such cases to the civil courts. So why should the army be any different?

Gopal Subramaniam, a member of the Justice Verma Committee, took a view which won widespread support, when he said that 'sexual offences by armed forces and uniformed men in conflict areas should be brought under ordinary criminal law'. After all, even the Supreme Court has declared that such acts cannot be defended as being 'in the line of duty'.

People's Police versus Policing the People

Harekrishna Deka

Till recently the Police Act, 1861 provided the legal framework for the police throughout India. A few states, including Assam, have recently adopted new laws but the 1861 Act is still in force in most states in the country. The 1861 Act has mentioned only one primary task for police in its preamble, the 'prevention and detection' of crime. The framing of various sections, however, makes it clear that maintenance of law and order was also one of its primary tasks. In fact during the Freedom Movement, the police forces of British India were extensively used as a coercive law and order force. I presume that 'keeping peace' comes within the ambit of law and order.

Section 13 of the Act speaks about deployment of additional forces for keeping peace. Section 14 allows even individuals and commercial concerns to requisition police for this purpose. Section 15, which envisages use of police in disturbed and dangerous districts, gives a law and order mandate to the police. Thus, according to this Act, the main role of the police is to combat crime and keep peace. This is abundantly clear from the text of this Act.

One has to remember that the Police Act was enacted by the Crown Raj in order not only to regulate an agency of the colonial government but also to keep the nation in subjugation. Provisions to regulate assembly of persons, quartering of additional forces in disturbed and dangerous districts, and imposition of collective fines on inhabitants of a disturbed area, all bear the stamp of this intention. The then central authority of the colonial government enforced this law uniformly throughout the country though the country had been divided into several provinces.

When the country became independent and policing became the responsibility of the states of the Indian Union, all states retained this law with minor modifications but without any fundamental change in the nature of policing. These minor modifications were made only to reflect the changed character of the new state governments. As a result, the sub-culture of the police continued without any change. When we talk of the role of police in the North-East we have to bear in mind that they are also the inheritors of this sub-culture and are not different in attitude, bearing, and perceptions from those of other Indian states. After Independence, police control just got transferred from a colonial administration to a political administration where the ruling party's interest became synonymous with the State's interest.

By specifying prevention and detection of crime as the police task, the Act gives police the responsibility of keeping a neighbourhood safe from criminal activities. The Indian penal code (IPC) and the criminal procedure code (CrPC) are the sources of their empowerment in this regard. But curiously, in this perception of security, the people have not been envisaged as a factor and there is no attempt in the Act to define the relationship between the people that forms a socio-economic community and the police that is tasked to secure an area inhabited by such a community. The words 'community' or 'people' do not appear anywhere in the Act. It may be that the colonialists deliberately avoided the use of these terms. There are mentions of 'person', 'inhabitant' and 'assembly', with negative connotations. These words appear in the context of potential violence and civic offences. The absence of the words 'community' and 'people' has made these terms overtaken by amnesia. The framers of the Act did not make any attempt to make the police community-conscious and, therefore, people's security is not a term that guides their actions. The psychological reflexes of police do not respond to this notion.

There is another Act enacted by the democratic government of India, i.e. the National Security Act (NSA) that speaks about 'security of the State'. But the State is apparently not coterminous with the people here either. It is aimed at containing the activities of potential trouble-mongers who may undermine the existing order of the State. Under this Act, the police are required to ensure security of the State but they are not required to be conscious of the people's security at the same time. The State is a structure of governance which in turn is the seat of power and the power is wielded by some people over others. The police force has all along been used as a tool in the hands of these powerful 'some'.

The higher formations of the police, that is, the gazetted officers, have been formed into different services after the country's independence. Interestingly, the word service was not used by the colonial government even for the higher formations. The Indian Police Service (IPS) was non-existent. There was only the Imperial Police (IP). It was no problem for the then government to call the highest bureaucratic service the Indian Civil Service (ICS) but they were weary of calling the imperial police a service. It was as if they wanted to avoid a relationship between the police and the community.

The Police Act of 1861 put a lot of emphasis on calling the police a force. The term 'police force' occurs in the act no less than 10 times between Sections 1 and 17. Section 2 clearly says, 'the entire police-establishment under a state government shall, for the purpose of this Act, be deemed to be one police force'. A force is an organised body of people and to that extent there is justification in calling police a force. But the word has other connotations which not only includes power and exerted strength but also in some context coercion or compulsion, especially with the use or threat of violence (Oxford English Reference Dictionary). Hence the negative connotations of the term 'force' should have been tempered by calling it a 'service' and its relationship with the community should have been established in a positive context, which is people's security. But this was desired by neither the colonial government nor the Indian government after Independence.

The force remained under the control of an impersonal administration and no attempt was made to give it a human face. The force has all along been used by the administration to police the people and not allowed to act as the people's police. It was thought politically expedient to maintain an invisible dividing line between the police of the state and its people. Although in the Act itself the word 'force' was used to imply that it was an organised body brought under a discipline for the purpose of preventing and detecting crime and also to prevent disturbance, the absence of any reference to the people and its subsequent use in a coercive manner programmed the force to deal with only the negative social situations. Moreover, the police were called an 'efficient instrument' (preamble) and not a human agency and thus human concerns were not incorporated in the psycho-frame of the Indian police.

The Indian police acquired a bad practice called 'third degree', an inhuman practice of torturing suspects to elicit information. Despite conscientious efforts by several senior police officers, this practice refuses to die. I feel that two reasons for the persistence of this practice are, (1) the dehumanisation of the force in its constitutional makeup springing from the provisions of the Police Act, 1861 itself and (2) the political culture that made it an instrument of coercive use.

Security has a larger dimension than just preventing and detecting crime. It has a qualitative aspect as well. Those who are given security have to feel that they are being protected and are not exposed to danger. If the 'instrument' constituted for the purpose of providing security fails to generate this psychological sense of security, there is a big lacuna in its constitution itself. Today, people's security is not in the vocabulary of police sub-culture—an inheritance of the colonial use of the force. When I say this I am speaking of the collective behaviour of a force always required to deal with the negative aspect of social behaviour and compelled to remain beholden to power-wielding political masters. Police sub-culture is not wedded to the society's value-based culture. In dealing with a stressful social situation they are programmed to look for potential trouble-mongers and their mind reacts accordingly. Many of the mishaps caused while dealing with public disturbance are not deliberate acts of police mischief, but are the fallout of the dehumanisation of the force in the framework of the law regulating them. Outside the uniform, a policeman may not be different in attitude from a common citizen but once he dons the uniform and becomes an element of the force he acts within the dehumanised sub-culture acquired by it.

It is not that there was never an intellectual effort to give the Indian police a new culture and spirit that fit the democratic values of the nation. The National Police Commission (NPC) constituted in 1977 under the chairmanship of Dharma Vira framed a model police bill for consideration of the government and expressly incorporated community-consciousness in the preamble of the proposed bill. It said, 'the police has a paramount obligation and duty to function according to the requirements of the constitution, law and the *democratic aspirations of the people.*' The bill also required police 'to be professional and *service-oriented* and free from extraneous influences and yet *accountable to the people*'. There was a clear attempt to incorporate the ingredients missing in the existing laws governing police functions. Unfortunately, the political mindset ruling the country has so far failed to transcend the political sub-culture it imbibed post-independence to serve narrow political ends and has allowed the proposed bill to go to oblivion.

As we come to the North-East scenario, we do not see any difference in the upbringing of police here since their sub-culture is a copy of the pan-Indian police sub-culture. Since they have been dealing with a complicated public order scenario for many decades, the absence of an equation between them and the people has been having a telling effect on their performance. When they fight insurgency they, of course, presume that they are fighting on behalf of the people. But the people do not feel so. The people feel that the fight is between the government forces and the insurgents and they are the victims of crossfire. For want of trust and consultation between the police and the community, the people, instead of accepting police as a people's force, treat them in the same footing as the insurgents—disturbers of peace and tranquility. This is an ironical situation.

The people often suffer from a sense of insecurity because of the violent activities of the insurgents. Yet they do not feel secure enough in the presence of the police because they tend to perceive a culture of violence in police actions too. In a pamphlet captioned 'Police Act 1861: Why we need to replace it', the Commonwealth Human Rights Initiative of New Delhi has rightly pointed out that 'policing in India has been by and large, a one sided affair with communities having little or no say in policing plans and strategies that affect them the most.' The pamphlet has pointed out that in South Africa the Constitution itself makes it the 'political responsibility of each province to promote good relations between the police and the community.' This promotes joint identification of problems and ensures joint responses to problem-solving. Ashutosh Varshney in his book *Ethnic Conflict and Civic Life*' has explained how civil society can play a major role in promoting ethnic peace. This applies also to all similar situations of human conflict. The police can succeed in providing security to the people only with the people's cooperation and not by distrusting them, nor remaining oblivious of them. The formulaic response of the police forces to the insurgency situation in the North-East has missed this ingredient and as a result instead of endeavoring to promote people's security, they are only fighting insurgency on behalf of a state apparatus.

The British officials themselves had found the police in British India corrupt. Remarks like 'unscrupulous in the exercise of their authority' and 'very general reputation for corruption and oppression' emanated from some of them only, but they did little to reform the police in India. In Assam, the late Anundoram Dhekial Phukan, a leading light of the Assamese society of the 19th century, found police so corrupt and inefficient that in his submission to A.J. Moffatt Mills, officiating judge, Sudder Court, Mymensing, he complained,

> We beg to submit that the police system of the country is wholly inefficient to preserve the lives and property of the people. The 'darogas' in the interior, to whose hands the Government has entrusted the duties of the police, fulfill their trust, with but few exceptions, without any justice either to themselves or to the people for whose protection they are entertained. That sordid practice which prevails among the ministerial officers of the courts prevails equally among the darogas.

Moffatt Mills in his report to Cecil Beadon, the then Secretary to the Government of Bengal disagreed with the remarks of Dhekial Phukan. Despite Moffat Mills' refutation, one can feel the popular perception of the time regarding the police system introduced by the British administration in Assam in those early days by reading Dhekial Phukan's report (Assam was then administratively a part of Bengal.). On the other hand, Moffat Mills' own remark reflected the typical attitude of a British official.

After Independence, the political class which assumed the mantle of the rulers of this country found it convenient to retain the same mould to suit their political ends. Only recently, at the intervention of the Supreme Court, which gave some binding directives to the central and state governments on hearing the petition of Prakash Singh and his associate, did the Government of India appoint a committee under the chairmanship of the noted lawyer, Soli Sorabjee, to draft a Model Police Act and circulated the draft Model Police Act to the state governments in 2006 for adopting a new state police law modeled on the draft Act. A few states did adopt a new Act, but after much dilution of the model Act, for example in Assam in 2007. In order to deprive the police of functional autonomy and retain a stranglehold over it, the directive of the Supreme Court to fix the tenure of the key police functionaries, particularly the police chief and the district police heads, to a minimum of two years has been ignored in this Act. The state, under political consideration, fixed the tenure of these key posts at one year with the rider that in 'public interest' the DGP and Superintendents of Police could be shifted at any time. In the prevailing political culture of this country, 'public interest' means politicians' interests. Moreover, though the draft Model Act made provisions for community liaison groups for each police station with participatory interest of the real stakeholders, i.e. the people taken into consideration, the new Assam Police Act simply found it not worthwhile.

At this point, we may refer to the following nine principles pronounced by Robert Peel for British police in the second decade of the 19th century.

1. The basic mission for which the police exist is to prevent crime and disorder.
2. The ability of police to perform their duties is dependent upon public approval of police action.
3. Police must secure the willing cooperation of the public in voluntary observance of the law to be able to secure and maintain the respect of the public.
4. The degree of cooperation that can be secured diminishes proportionately to the necessity of the use of the physical force.
5. Police seek and preserve public favour not by catering to public opinion but by constantly demonstrating absolute impartial service to the law.
6. Police use physical force to the extent necessary to secure observance of the law or to restore order only when the

exercise of persuasion, advice, and warning is found to be insufficient.

7. Police, at all times, should maintain a relationship with the public that gives reality to the historic tradition that the police are the public and the public are the police; the police being the only members of the public who are paid to give full-time attention to duties which are incumbent on every citizen in the interest of community welfare and existence.
8. Police should always direct their actions strictly towards their functions and never appear to usurp the powers of the judiciary.
9. The test of police efficiency is the absence of crime and order, not the visible evidence of police action in dealing with it.

These principles were enunciated by Robert Peel for British Police much before the colonial Police Act, 1861 was enacted by the British Raj for the police administration in India. The colonial administration had deliberately ignored these principles while enacting the Indian Police Act as they wanted an agency to suppress the democratic aspirations of their Indian subjects. In Assam's new Police Act also, some of these principles get ignored as these are found to be politically inconvenient.

Speaking about democratic policing, an American scholar Jerome H. Skolnick remarked, 'democratic police forces are not supposed to be insular, self-contained, or cut-off from the communities from which their power derives.' (Democratic Policing, Police Foundation, August 1999).

The new 21st century Assam Police Act falls short of a democratic police philosophy as it keeps the force under political shackles and also fails to create a workable police–public institutional interface. Most unfortunately, the need for community policing fails to receive due attention of the policy-makers though some of its aspects find mention in a diffused way in the Act. There is a Village Defense Organisation in Assam with volunteers drawn from the villages, mainly to assist police in rural policing by way of mounting night vigilance and conducting night patrols in their own villages, but they do not represent the rural community as such and do not articulate the community's opinions on issues of social interest involving security of the society as a whole.

There is only a cosmetic effort to create social consciousness amongst police personnel by way of incorporating a section in the Assam Police Act, 2007 in a perfunctory manner. There has been no effort to make much-needed structural changes in the force or to prepare its human resources providing for a training methodology without any mismatch between professional needs and the social value-system, without which not much change can be brought about in the police sub-culture inherited from the colonial past.

The new Assam Police Act fails to address these requirements. One structural change needed is either to do away with the post of constables, as they are used like waste-products although they form the bulk of the force, or to assign some productive functions to them after raising their quality and attitude through appropriate training programmes. Moreover, the Act speaks of police accountability without allowing functional autonomy. Thus many provisions of the Model Police Act, 2006 intended to radically change police philosophy were sidetracked or diluted in this state statute.

Having mentioned of police philosophy above, I will like to say that a *police philosophy* should have the following elements:

1. *Professionalism.* It should get reflected in a policeperson's attitude to work, in his/her conduct in public, his/her sense of purpose, his/her integrity and honesty, or his/her regard to a standard of performance. He/she should be sensitive to the cultural values of the people and responsive to the community in providing legitimate services. He/she must be effective in fighting crime to earn respect and feel proud of his/her work.
2. *Accountability.* To whom are police accountable? All members of a police force are accountable to the State through the disciplinary

and command structure of the force but within the framework of the rule of law and not beyond that. Besides, though the police have been called a force, there has to be a clear understanding that police provide service to the community and that they are responsible for securing human life and property, that they are the representatives of the people and, therefore, are accountable to the people. As Robert Peel said, 'police are people and people are police'.

3. *Respect for human rights.* It is disquieting that 60 per cent of complaints against police received by National Human Rights Commission (NHRC) are of human rights abuses. The police personnel in the lower rank are not even aware of the existence of something like the Protection of Human Rights Act, 1993. Many of them routinely abuse human rights thinking that the uniform gives them immunity.
4. *Operational responsibility.* In a political system, police cannot have operational freedom from political executive. But they have operational responsibilities. To fulfill their operational responsibilities, they should function in a system where they are free from all extraneous influences in their professional roles.
5. *Impartiality.* It is not just that police themselves feel that they are impartial but they must be seen to be impartial in discharge of their duties.

Police philosophy based on the above elements should be enunciated clearly as a *statement of principles* in the working manuals of the police force. In Assam, though a new Act is in force since a few years now, the old manuals are still in use despite the legal requirement that new rules/manuals under the current law should have been framed and enforced. Assam police has a new law but no rules drawn from the provisions of this law. It does not have a clearly enunciated philosophy.

Coming to police reform, the first question is where does it start? I have no doubt that the Police station should be the focal point of police reforms because that is the first contact point between the police and the people. If there is a trust deficit in police in public mind, it starts here. Certain deficiencies need to be taken note of.

Deficiencies in Implementation of Police Reforms

1. A small staff has to look after a very large area. (Police–population ratio in India is 129 to 1 lakh)
2. Police is so preoccupied with law and order duties that investigation of crime is neglected. Often, preoccupation with law and order is taken as a pretext for neglecting crime.
3. In the political situation prevailing in the country, political acceptability has become the criterion for posting an officer at a police station rather than his/her professional competence or actual performance.
4. There is no established system of compulsory refresher training. After the initial training, most police officers end their career without seeing a training institute except when they are required to attend the promotion cadre course, organised generally in a routine and perfunctory manner.
5. Recruitment procedures are not transparent and in most states it is not done on merit but on political recommendations or by bribing. Because of lack of transparency, corrupt practices in transfer and postings are rampant. Some posts are considered 'lucrative' and these postings carry a price. As a result, the quality of human resource suffers.
6. There is no satisfactory mechanism for police–public interface. As a result, neither the police understand the society's security requirements nor do the people understand the difficulties of the force.
7. The beat system has been stopped due to inadequate manpower. Much of their time and energy are spent on VIP security duties. The beat system is a very useful way of gaining local knowledge, understanding the prevailing social climate, remaining visible,

gaining familiarity with citizens, and collecting criminal intelligence. Each police station should have a number of beats, properly notified, and sufficient manpower must be sanctioned for police stations taking beats into account.

8. For prompt response, police need dependable communication and transport facilities. In most police stations, they do with outdated communication equipment and transport. There is no established system of periodic review for modernising these. Police is also slow in adapting new technology. Criminal world has been outpacing the police in the use of technology.
9. Although bulk of the staff in a police station comprise of constables, they hardly perform useful duty. The colonial government did not want to assign any important duty to the constables. The Police Commission of 1902 wanted that the 'duties of a police constable should be of mechanical character' and 'duties requiring discretion and judgment' should not be entrusted to them. There is no change of perception even now in this regard and there is a huge waste of manpower.
10. Police in India is reactive, not proactive. They respond after an event has taken place. The approach to crime has to change to a preventive–proactive mode.
11. Majority of police stations do not have a cell staffed by women police officers. Women are uncomfortable in opening up before male police officers.

The new Assam Police Act has failed to address many of these requirements. The state needs to think of amending the Act to make it a proper framework for democratic policing.

Police reform should have a new emphasis on 'active participation of civil society' as was declared by the Commonwealth Heads of Government Meeting in 2003. Sir John Stevens, former Commissioner of the London Metropolitan Police, said, 'Central to identifying problems and the solutions to local crime and disorder issues is effective community consultation.... An organization that truly reflects the needs of communities will inspire the trust and confidence and support of the people it serves.'

(This paper was earlier presented in a seminar at Guwahati University. An abridged version of this was published in Akhil Ranjan Dutta (ed). 2009. *Human Security in North-East India: Issues and Policies*)

Small Arms Proliferation in the North-East: The Chinese Connection

Rajeev Bhattacharyya

The illicit proliferation and misuse of small arms are among the most pressing security threats affecting several countries. Thousands of people are killed and/or wounded every year in conflicts fought primarily with these weapons. Proliferation of small arms has gradually increased in the Indian subcontinent fuelled by a host of factors including spread of low intensity conflicts. India's north-east is one of the most affected zones since the maximum number of insurgent outfits are found in this region. In addition, a variety of transnational criminal activities have increased in the region which increased the demand for small arms. Such demand for small arms is matched by an equally prompt supply from different sources supported by an intricate web of relations and agreements that cut across regions, communities, and countries. The failure of governments to come together and chalk out coordinated efforts adds to the problem.

Definition

Ambiguity shrouds the definition of small arms. The United Nations, in an agreement reached in 2005, has defined small arms and light weapons as any 'man-portable lethal weapon that expels or launches, or designed to expel or launch, or may be readily converted to expel or launch a shot, bullet, or projectile by the action of an explosive.' It adds that a small arm is a weapon designed for individual use that include, inter alia, revolvers and self-loading pistols, rifles and carbines, sub-machine guns, assault rifles, and light machine guns.

Weapons may be designed for use by two or three persons serving as a crew but some may be carried and used by a single person. They include heavy machine guns, hand-held under-barrel and mounted grenade launchers, portable anti-aircraft guns, portable anti-tank guns, recoilless rifles, portable launchers of anti-tank missile and rocket systems, portable launchers of anti-aircraft missile systems and mortars of a caliber less than 100 mm.[1]

According to another definition, any firearm that can be fired by the hand and whose caliber is below 12.67 mm is called a small arm.

India's north-east and adjoining areas have witnessed proliferation of not only small arms but grenades as well which are in fact more easily available. Supply of Chinese arms through Bangladesh has somewhat become irregular since 2006 (which is why the Myanmar routes have become more active) after the military backed regime assumed power in Dhaka. As such, a discussion on arms proliferation would be incomplete without including grenades which in fact have been used more frequently than small arms in attacks by militants in the northeast. The two items are inseparable as both are ferried by the same agents along the same routes and released from the same destinations barring a few exceptions.

The Problem

New Delhi's so-called multi-pronged approach to tackle insurgency in the North-East, which is intricately related to the increasing demand for small arms, suffers from fundamental flaws. For one, not all movements in the region are imbued with a separatist hue but essentially the outcome of unemployment and alienation. The outfits in Assam's hill districts and those from the Kuki–Chin–Mizo communities in Manipur and Mizoram are glaring examples.

A majority of them has already come overground through ceasefire agreements with the government. So unemployment should be tackled on a war footing, developmental projects completed in a time-bound manner and greater transparency ensured at all levels of administration. Allocation of development funds has been increased in all states in the region but embezzlement continues unabated. Scams are dug out at regular intervals. On 30 May 2009, Mohit Hojai, the chief executive member of North Cachar Hills Autonomous Council (NCHAC) in Assam, was arrested along with R.H. Khan, a joint director, for misappropriation of development funds and sharing those with militants. (The case is being examined by the National Investigation Agency).

Similarly, there have been no attempts to comprehend the problem of small arms proliferation in the region and its linkages with the hotspots in China and south-east Asian countries. Therefore, there have been no sustained efforts to work out a solution. The problem indeed is very serious. If available facts are taken into account, such as the sale of firearms are sold at hubs across Assam, Manipur, Nagaland, Arunachal Pradesh, and Meghalaya. One needs to have only the right contacts to buy sophisticated assault rifles and grenades. And a good majority of the arms consignments is released from Yunnan province in China and distributed in the entire region through a well-organised network sustained mainly by the military–militant–mafia nexus.

But who are the actual players in this illicit trade? Is Beijing involved or is it solely criminal gangs that have targeted the North-East as a lucrative destination? Why are Chinese firearms more easily available now compared to a decade ago? And what is the quantity of such firearms available in the region?

The government's awareness and attitude to the problem is best revealed by the contradictory responses received from the Union and Assam governments on confiscation of Chinese arms and grenades between 1997 and 2007. Response to an application filed by the author under the Right to Information (RTI) Act with MHA said that a total of 34 items were seized in Assam during the 10-year period that included 20 pistols but no grenades. Data given by the state government says that 204 grenades, 41 pistols and 42 assault rifles (AK 47 and AK 56) were confiscated in seven districts of Assam alone during the same period[2]. A senior journalist from Manipur also cast serious doubts on the figures given on Manipur by MHA[3]. The same pattern would undoubtedly emerge if data is gathered from the rest of the north-eastern states.

Table 1: Chinese-made Firearms and Grenades Seized during 1997–2007 as per Ministry of Home Affairs

Year	Assam	Manipur	Meghalaya	Punjab	Uttar Pradesh	West Bengal	Delhi	Total
1997	9						1	10
1998	10							10
1999	8							8
2000					4	1	1	6
2001							1	1
2002	2				1			3
2003			6		8		1	15
2004	1		7		1			9
2005	3		6					9
2006							1	1
2007	**1**	**1**		**4**				**6**
Total	**34**	**1**	**19**	**4**	**14**	**1**	**5**	**78**

Source: Union Ministry of Home Affairs, in response to a query under RTI.

Confiscated Chinese-made Firearms and Grenades in Assam

An estimated 75 million firearms exist in South Asia, 63 million of which are in unauthorised hands[4]. The North-East became a market for illegal arms ever since the Naga National Council (NNC) raised the banner of revolt in the mid-1950s. From a few rifles given by China in the late 1960s to NNC, the sources expanded over the years and they have been traced to Pakistan, USA, UK, Czechoslovakia, Afghanistan, Bangladesh, Cambodia, Myanmar, and Israel[5]. During the last decade or so, supply of Chinese made firearms in the area has far exceeded other countries. This aspect has been proved from the seizures made and from interrogation of gunrunners and militants.

Table 2: Data on Confiscated Chinese-made Firearms and Grenades from Assam during 1997–2007 As Per Assam Government

District	Grenades	Pistols	AK 47 and AK 56 Assault Rifles	Total
Kokrajhar		1	2	3
Dhubri	6	1	14	21
Sivasagar	3			3
Karbi Anglong	26	11	14	51
Kamrup	17	8	3	28
Baksa	102	15	2	119
Odalguri	50	5	7	62
Total	204	41	42	287

Source: Assam government, in response to a query under RTI.

There is, however, no evidence to suggest that the Chinese government is directly involved in the illicit trade. Release of firearms and grenades in a manner that discerns the official stamp is difficult. A senior official in MHA said,

> We have asked the Ministry of External Affairs several times to take it up with Beijing but they have time and again told us to provide hard evidence which is next to impossible. So we have stopped bothering ourselves. Ultimately MEA has a

> role to play in checking the menace and it can't simply put the blame on us.[6]

Not only that, intelligence agencies drew flak when they were asked by the Prime Minister's Office (PMO) to submit details in 2008.

Firearms are not produced by private agencies in China. The state-owned Norinco is among the top five manufacturers of rifles, sub-machine guns, machine guns, and grenade launchers in the world. The others are Heckler and Koch in Germany, Izhmash in Russia, Colt in USA, and F.N. Herstel in Belgium. According to available data and estimates, the Russian Federation, USA, Italy, Germany, Brazil, and China *exported* small arms and light weapons worth more than US $ 100 million in 2003.[7] Not surprisingly, it is not only India's north-east that has been flooded with Chinese firearms; the Taliban is using them and the People's Liberation Army of Nepal also had access to sources in China.

Most militant outfits are ignorant about the nuances of the trade barring some in Manipur and Nagaland. Many are, however, aware that consignments mostly originate in China. The author saw a few M 16 rifles in Manipur with cadres of the United Kuki Liberation Front (UKLF), Kuki Liberation Army (KLA), and People's Liberation Army (PLA). But the bulk was undeniably the Chinese-made Kalashnikov assault rifle and 9 mm pistol. A few assault rifles even have two Chinese alphabets marked on them meaning 'Lian Dan', an automatic rifle or something that can shoot continuously.[8] It is difficult to imagine that assault rifles produced in a country other than China would have these alphabets. However, since 2009, there are reports suggesting that the Kachin Independence Army (KIA) has begun producing assault rifles in Myanmar based on Chinese designs.[9]

Similar to the arms haul of 2 April 2004 in Chittagong, Bangladesh, another episode had occurred in the icy heights of the Sino–Bhutan border in 1997, but in a smaller scale. Information reached Indian intelligence agencies that a consignment belonging to United Liberation Front of Asom (ULFA), National Democratic Front of Bodoland (NDFB), and Kamtapur Liberation Organization (KLO), was waiting to be transported from China to camps in southern Bhutan. Thimpu was alerted. Not only was the entire operation foiled but three Bhutanese army officials who colluded with the rebels were arrested and put behind bars.[10]

Senior leaders belonging to United People's Democratic Solidarity (UPDS) and ULFA's 28th Battalion (A and C Companies) have stated that around 70–80 per cent of their armoury of assault rifles, pistols, cartridges, grenades, and grenade launchers are of Chinese origin.[11] It is not without reason that the Communist Party of India (Maoist) active in central India has firmed up an alliance with Manipur's PLA last year.[12] With the left-wing insurgency drawing to a close in Nepal and LTTE's base demolished in Sri Lanka, a viable option for supply of firearms could be from China through the North-East. PLA is one of the outfits believed to have a presence in Yunnan and some pockets along the Sino–Myanmar border.

The demand has increased over the years and arms will continue to pour into the North-East since there is no sanction of any sort on any of the supplier countries. Unlike other weapons, no international control system governs small arms and grenades. During the Cold War, nuclear, biological, and chemical weapons dominated international policy agendas and arms control efforts. Until the early 1990s, if countries were interested in the control of conventional weapons, it was predominantly heavy weapons that received attention. The UN Register of Conventional Arms—a voluntary mechanism for sharing information on imports, exports, and procurement of some weapons systems—and the Wassenaar arrangement to promote greater responsibility in conventional arms and dual use exports, focus primarily on heavy conventional weapons. Small arms were often left out of these initiatives. All that the UN has been able to achieve so far are a set of three international instruments—the politically-binding Programme of Action adopted in July 2001; the legally-binding Protocol Against Illicit Manufacturing of and Trafficking in Firearms, Their Parts and Components and Ammunition, which came into force on 3 July 2005; and the politically-binding International Instrument to Enable States to Identify and Trace, in a Timely and Reliable Manner, Illicit Small Arms and Light Weapons—adopted by the General Assembly in December 2005. These Protocols are limited in scope and content and they set standards for national systems in such areas as firearms manufacture, marking, and transfer.

Causes of Proliferation

A combination of several factors has made the North-East and adjacent regions ideal for transnational crimes like gunrunning and drug trafficking. They are fuelled by a distinct set of push and pull factors ranging from policies followed by Chinese ordnance factories to the volatile situation in Myanmar, Bangladesh, and north-east India.

President Deng Xiaoping, the architect of China's vibrant economy today, had directed the military to generate its own resources. The Peoples' Liberation Army (of China) had reportedly even run night clubs for self-sustenance![13] Over a period of time, Norinco, the state-run ordnance factory, began selling arms to buyers from different countries. This explains the widespread availability of Chinese firearms in all troubled spots in Central and South Asia. It was also in the late 1990s that some mafia groups (like Blackhouse) in Yunnan began supplying these weapons from ordnance factories to North-East rebels.[14] The biggest advantage of this source was that firearms were much cheaper than Thailand's and supply through land routes in Myanmar more consistent and safer than sea routes.

Easy availability led some outfits like PLA and ULFA to station their own agents permanently in a few Chinese towns close to Kachin in Myanmar. After Operation All Clear in Bhutan in 2003, ULFA dispatched a small team under SS Lt Partha Gogoi to establish a liaison office near Putao on the Sino–Myanmar border.

ULFA Chief of Staff Paresh Baruah visited this office and even held a meeting with Burmese and Chinese army officials in late 2005. Subsequently the ULFA supremo slipped into Yunnan in China and stayed there for a few months. This was exposed by a TV news channel on the day of the serial blasts in Assam on 30 October 2008. This was also later confirmed by former Director General of Assam Police G.M. Srivastava.[15]

Surprising as it may seem in a country ruled with an iron fist, the situation in some areas of Yunnan is not very different from India's north-east or some areas of Myanmar's in so far as law and order is concerned. Describing the state of affairs in the province in 1995, a leading Asian magazine said, 'Last year seizures of illegal arms were up nearly 30 per cent over 1993. That reflected both increasing availability of guns and rising official alarm. In September, a month-long crackdown netted some 120,000 illegal weapons. While military handguns are the hottest item, gunrunning syndicates are also marketing grenades and sub-machine guns. In May 1995, Guangdong police seized anti-tank rocket launchers. It goes on to explain how firearms once sold to Vietnamese and Myanmarese communists by Beijing were finding their way back to Yunnan and landing in the hands of organized crime syndicates.[16]

The task of these crime syndicates has been rendered easier by the existing conditions in Bangladesh and Myanmar that facilitated a military–militant–mafia nexus and easy availability of porters and agents due to unemployment and poverty. In Bangladesh though, Pakistan's ISI was an important factor and its role has been reconfirmed from the new investigation into the Chittagong arms haul of 2 April 2004. Two senior officials from National Security Intelligence (Bangladesh equivalent of Intelligence Bureau), have also been arrested. The interrogation of a local gunrunner Hafizur Rehman has revealed that ULFA's Paresh Baruah and Anthony Shimray, intelligence chief of NSCN (IM), were present when the consignment came in from the Sittwe Port in Myanmar by sea. This consignment too was sourced from Yunnan and many North-East outfits and the CPI (Maoist) had a stake in it.

In Myanmar, the lure of easy money has drawn a section of Myanmarese army officials into drug trafficking and other illicit trades.[17] At least two of the 20 odd insurgent outfits, KIA and United Wa State Army (UWSA), that arrived at ceasefire agreements with the Myanmarese Junta, have forged links with Yunnan and the mafia to get a share in the arms trade. Incidentally all these insurgent groups have been allowed to carry out all kinds of activities in their respective territories by the government. A ban on opium cultivation has been imposed in Kokang and Wa regions in Myanmar but it has had the unintended consequence of enhancing poverty and forcing people into gunrunning and production of synthetic drugs as a means of alternate livelihood.

UWSA deserves a special mention as it is both the largest ethnic and narco-ethnic army in the region with a strength of more than 20,000.[18] Wa soldiers formed the bulk of the Communist Party of Burma (CPB) till they revolted and decided to float the present organisation in 1989. Today it has monopolised the entire trade on amphetamine (a synthetic drug or ATS) and some of its leaders like the Wei brothers are among the biggest drug barons in Myanmar. The US has indicted as many as eight senior Wa leaders on drug trafficking charges including Bao You Chang, chairman of United Wa State Party, the political front of UWSA.

UWSA cadres have been spotted at Tamu across Moreh in Manipur and there has since been an increasing inflow of 'yaba' (ATS variant) into Manipur. They have firmed up deals with Naga and Kuki rebels and are also the main suppliers of weapons in a huge stretch along the Chandel–Churachandpur belt.[19] Chinese officials have welcomed Wa investment in Yunnan; the Golden Phoenix Hotel in Simao is proudly described as a joint venture between 'the Wa Federation of Myanmar [Burma]' and Yunnan's Provincial Farming Bureau.[20]

Like the Wa troops, many North-East militant groups have also taken to gunrunning and protection of the drug trade albeit on a lesser scale. Both the Isak–Muivah and Khaplang factions of NSCN, UNLF, PLA, Prepak, Kanglei Yawol Kanna Lup (KYKL), Zomi Revolutionary Association (ZRA), and Kuki National Association (KNA) are allegedly among some groups that are involved. They tax all drugs and arms consignments passing through their areas. Since extortion from businessmen and government officials does not amount to much in the hill states, extra income is needed from other sources to pay allowances to cadres and for operations. Interestingly, the annual expenses of many outfits have gone up after they signed ceasefire agreements with the Centre.[21] Most of these groups have recruited more cadres after coming overground in violation of the ceasefire agreement. Young adults and children are always available for these operations due to rampant unemployment, socio-economic deprivation, and a host of other factors.

Hubs, Routes and Rates

Most of the consignments used to originate in Thailand which receive arms from China and Cambodia. Ships with arms would reach Cox Bazar and other regions of Chittagong. The arms were then taken to different destinations in the North-East. Sonamura in Tripura, Jayantia and Garo Hills in Meghalaya, and Dhubri in Assam were the favoured entry points for supply to NSCN (IM), ULFA, and Bodo and Manipuri rebels. But two incidents in 1995–96, Operation Golden Bird by Indian army in Mizoram and a mysterious blast in a ship carrying weapons, shifted the focus to the overland and riverine routes through Myanmar as safer and less time consuming. Added to this was the tough posture against militants and gunrunners by the army-backed regime that assumed power in Dhaka in 2006 and the current Awami League led government that ruptured the earlier congenial ambience for these activities in Bangladesh. In late 2009, NSCN (IM)'s intelligence chief Anthony Shimray procured weapons from Yunnan which he wanted to transport through Bangladesh. The Directorate General of Forces Intelligence (DGFI) refused permission. Subsequently the consignment had to be taken to the Buthidaung jetty on the banks of the Mayu river in Myanmar and from there to different locations.[22]

Deals are struck at Ruili in Yunnan but another town Tengchong in the same province in China is where consignments are released to be sent across Myanmar to select spots along the Indo–Myanmar border.[23] These two routes branch off into different directions in Myanmar. Even the Irrawady and Chindwin rivers are now being used profusely for faster passage. A senior NSCN (K) cadre said his chairman S.S. Khaplang derives a regular income by taxing boats that ferry arms through the Chindwin. Consignments are offloaded and arms stacked at some points (like Tamu) till orders are received from the North-East. Phek in Nagaland, Chandel, and Churachanpur in Manipur and Champai in Mizoram are the entry points to other destinations in the region.

It is a common refrain among Indian army and police officials that NSCN and Kuki militants often go to Myanmar empty handed and return laden with arms. If caught, they would simply say that the weapons were from the designated ceasefire camps and usually no case is made out against them. There have also been several cases when NSCN cadres have sold arms and ammunition to Dimasa militants. They sometimes stole arms from the armoury at Camp Hebron near Dimapur.[24] Individual agents also sometimes make direct purchases from these villages and sell it elsewhere. On 25 July 2009, two Naga youths, Akam Konyak and Tinkam Konyak, were arrested at Namtola in Sivasagar district of Assam after they were caught trying to sell a pistol to a customer.

Routes inside India keep on changing and they pass through National Highways, forests, hilly terrain, and towns. The heavy deployment of security forces along the Moreh–Imphal–Kohima–Dimapur highway has made the other road that originates at

Champhai in Mizoram and passes through Silchar–Ladrymbai–8 Mile–Umrangsho–Jirikinding–Panimur Waterfalls (after crossing Kopili River)–NC Hills more important. At times, small quantities may be offloaded at Jirikinding in Karbi Anglong district of Assam to be taken to other destinations. Agents are found at selected towns and villages along the way or nearby areas who would place the order either at Moreh or Dimapur, the biggest hotspots in the North-East for purchase of arms. In NC Hills, a well known arms dealer, Nambui Dumgbe, was shot dead by Black Widow militants at Tumje on 17 March 2009 since he had sold weapons to a rival faction.

The network is sustained by a delicate understanding among militant groups, agents, and sometimes government officials. Quite often a group might ask for a part of the consignment as fees for taking them from one point to another and allowing passage through the territories they dominate. The United National Liberation Front (UNLF) colluded with the Myanmarese Chin National Front (CNF) to procure weapons from different destinations and two major deliveries were received in 1996 and 1998.

The price goes higher as the consignment(s) travel deeper into North-East. For instance, an AK 47 assault rifle costs between ₹ 2.5 to 2.7 lakh in Moreh-Tamu which could go up to ₹ 3 lakh and even higher by the time it reaches NC Hills. Among all items, the rates at which 9 mm pistols are sold have been found to fluctuate. An original Chinese made pistol is as expensive as ₹ 2 lakh and as less as ₹20,000 for assembled pieces. This cheap variety is sold in pockets in some villages from NC Hills to Changlang in Arunachal Pradesh.

Table 3: Cost of Firearms/Grenades (₹)

Item	Moreh-Tamu	NC Hills and Karbi Anglong
AK 47/56	2.5 to 2.7 lakh	3 to 3.15 lakh
9 mm pistol	1.3 to 1.5 lakh	2.2 to 2.8 lakh
Grenade	6,000 to 7,000	5,000 to 8,000

Ammunition of AK 47/56	230 to 250 (per cartridge)	275 to 300 (per cartridge)
Ammunition of 9 mm pistol	100 to 120 (per cartridge)	120 to 150 (per cartridge)

It is reported that apart from pistols, assault rifles are assembled at Moreh and Saikul in Manipur. These are made of spare parts obtained from Myanmar and local manufacturers. The cost of an AK 47 produced at these centres range between ₹ 1.5 to 1.7 lakh and is sometimes sold as Chinese make. Dimasa and Kuki militants, who have used them, said their quality was inferior as the barrel gets heated up fast. There is problem with the magazine as well. But the demand for these seems to be picking up with the emergence of more and more gangs with a stake in different types of transnational crimes.

Stemming the Flow

Growing criminalisation and proliferation of small arms and grenades are vexing problems, the prevention of which calls for a multi-layered approach and coordination among all agencies. India has broached the issue of arms proliferation many a time with Beijing. The situation has, however, only deteriorated with the illegal trade showing an increase in volume over the past few years. However, what has been encouraging for India was a statement by Li Baodong, Chinese representative to the UN, on 20 March 2010, that his country was opposed to the illicit production and proliferation of small arms. Li, who was speaking with reference to the Central African region, pointed out that China was willing to work along with the international community towards an 'early and appropriate' solution to the problem. 'Each state should, on the basis of the UN Program of Action on Small Arms and in connection with its specific situation, formulate a complete set of rules and regulations on the production, possession, transfer and stockpile of small arms and ensure their effective enforcement', he said at an open debate of the Security Council and added that countries of the region

(Central Africa) should strengthen coordination and cooperation to monitor trade in small arms and combat illicit transactions.

Li's statement is a heartening departure since China, as well as US and Russia, have always been opposed to certain measures long advocated by non-governmental organisations (NGOs) and other think-tanks across the globe that could have made a dent in the scale of the unlawful trade. Laws like legally-binding international treaties on arms brokering, development of transparency mechanisms for exports and imports of small arms and expansion of programmes of assistance to states seeking more effective implementation are being contested by some countries due to the apprehension that such initiatives would encroach upon their national practices and limit their future freedom of action. NGOs have, in particular, made a case for marking and tracing of weapons since it is difficult to ascertain their origin, which countries they travelled through, and where they were being used. If the origin and transfer routes of weapons can be verified, it would be much easier to work out how and when they got into the hands of unintended users and identify those responsible for supplying and diverting the arms. The marking of small arms is, to some extent, covered by the UN Firearms Protocol. But there is no single system for marking or tracing small arms. A few NGOs, led by Groupe de Recherche et d'information sur la paix et la securite have developed a draft convention (Draft Convention on Marking, Registration and Tracing of Small Arms and Light Weapons: Grounds for Action and Overview of the Articles) that addresses some of these concerns.

The debate on proliferation has also focused on limiting the impact of weapons currently in circulation which would perhaps hold true for the situation at Yunnan in China and Myanmar. Surplus weapons existing in a country can easily find their way to the black market. For example, an Ukrainian parliamentary commission estimated that when the country achieved independence in 1992, its military stocks were worth $ 89 billion. Over the next decade thousands of these weapons were stolen and sold abroad, including to governments and insurgent groups, in several war zones. Therefore, government weapons stockpiles must be effectively managed and secured. Disarmament, demobilisation, and reintegration (DDR) programmes often help to reduce the illicit trafficking and misuse of weapons in the hands of ex-combatants and armed gangs. In the North-East, militant groups that have signed accords and ceasefire agreements with the government have never surrendered their entire arsenal but have either sold them to other groups or stacked them for possible future use.

The situation in South and South-East Asia is somewhat different from other war zones. India could, therefore, make efforts to develop a consensus at fora such as SAARC and ASEAN and initiate dialogues with countries of the region affected by small arms proliferation. The objective should be to identify deficiencies in national arms control policies and to bring about remedial measures within a stipulated timeframe. China must be pressurised to change its policies to ensure firm control over ordnance factories as well as weapons issued to the military and police. Equally of concern for the North-East is the situation in and role of the dictatorial regime in Myanmar. With reports pouring in on the establishment of an arms manufacturing factory by the militants, proliferation would still continue even if the supply routes from China are blocked. With Myanmar dictator General Than Shwe cozying up with India, New Delhi must seize the opportunity to drive home the point that curbing transnational crimes like gun-running would stand to benefit both countries in the long run. Of course, it is true that unless poverty is reduced in Myanmar and a final settlement is reached with militant outfits like KIA or UWSA, a change in government policy may not have the desired result.

Since India is already investing on infrastructure in Myanmar, the policy could well be expanded to include Sagaing and Kachin adjacent to the North-East having a direct bearing on small arms proliferation. These twin regions are the least developed in Myanmar with deplorable social and economic infrastructure. This also explains the involvement of the local populace in transnational criminal activities. Besides opening up vistas of employment, development of Kachin and Sagaing would also be in sync with India's Look East Policy to reach out to and establish a bridge with south-east Asia. In fact, Nagaland chief minister Neiphiu Rio has already taken up the issue with the Centre and has made a case for New Delhi's active involvement in 'eastern Nagaland' (Sagaing) which he described as 'no man's land'. Investments apart, New Delhi must also consider fencing the Indo–Myanmar border on the lines of Indo–Bangla border to curb illegal trade. A review of the free border regime that allows free movement of people on both sides of the Indo–Myanmar border must be reviewed and restrictions imposed in vulnerable zones. Appropriate number of Assam Rifles personnel must be deputed for border policing which may necessitate raising additional manpower. Local communities on both sides of the border must be made aware of the ill-effects of gunrunning. Assistance of credible NGOs must be accepted wherever essential. Above all, development of border areas must be taken up on a war-footing so that alienation is curbed and employment avenues are opened up. To a considerable extent, increase in gunrunning in the North-East is the direct fallout of decades of negligence of the frontier regions.

Conclusion

China is the primary origin of arms and grenades that are released and distributed through a highly systematic and discreet network with little evidence to pinpoint Beijing's role. Myanmar, Bangladesh, and Thailand to an extent, are routes for small arms. A large number of people in these countries and the North-East, including government officials, militants, and the mafia, benefit from small arms proliferation that seems to have grown in volume in the past decade. New Delhi must have a comprehensive and holistic policy on small arms. Moreover, there is an urgent need to expand the definition of small arms to include grenades. Small arms proliferation is not confined to North-East but they reach other parts of India as well. But security forces and agencies have not been able to comprehend the gravity of the problem or about its dangerous implications. Furthermore, little effort has been made so far to have a serious dialogue on the issue with neighbouring countries. Therefore, the possibility of a slide in the inflow of small arms and grenades looks a remote possibility in the near future.

Notes

1. Adopted by United Nations General Assembly on 8 December 2005 and included in the International Instrument to Enable States to Identify and Trace, in a Timely and Reliable Manner, Illicit Small Arms and Light Weapons.
2. Application filed by the author under Right to Information Act with Assam Police on 25 June 2009.
3. Pradeep Phanjoubam's remark in the seminar on Small Arms Proliferation held at Omeo Kumar Das Institute for Social Change and Development, Guwahati, on 18 June 2009.
4. Mandy Turner and Bina Lakshmi Nepram. The Impact of Armed Violence in North East India: A Mini Case Study for the Armed Violence and Poverty Initiative. November 2004. Centre for International Cooperation and Security.
5. Mandy Turner and Bina Lakshmi Nepram. The Impact of Armed Violence in North East India: A Mini Case Study for the Armed Violence and Poverty Initiative. November 2004. Centre for International Cooperation and Security.
6. Discussions with a director in the Ministry of Home Affairs on 3 January 2008.
7. 'Small Arms Survey', Graduate Institute of International Studies, Geneva, 2006.
8. These alphabets were seen on some AK 56 rifles with cadres of United Peoples' Democratic Solidarity (UPDS) cadres at Rongbin in Karbi Anglong and at Sinai in Chandel with United Kuki Liberation Front (UKLF) cadres.
9. Interview of journalist and author Bertil Lintner on 23 February 2013 in Guwahati.
10. Interview with ULFA militants and intelligence officials in 2004 after Operation All Clear in Bhutan in December 2003.
11. Interview with Mrinal Hazarika (former commandant of ULFA's 28th Battalion) on 2 November 2008 and Lengbat Ingleng (Defence Secretary of UPDS) on 31 January 2008.
12. Manohar Mayum, Commander-in-Chief of Peoples' Liberation Army (PLA)

told about the alliance with Naxalites to journalists in one of their camps on Indo–Myanmar border near Ukhrul in Manipur on 4 May 2009.

13. Interview with a Joint Secretary in the Research and Analysis Wing (RAW) on 5 December 2007.
14. Interview with a surrendered functionary of ULFA on 1 November 2010.
15. 'Serial Blasts Rock Assam', *Times Now,* 30 October 2008.
16. 'Law and Disorder: A Growing Torrent of Guns and Narcotics Overwhelms China'. Anthony Davis. *Asia Week,* 25 August 1995.
17. 'Transnational Crime in Burma'. Liana Sun Wyler. CRS Report for Congress, 29 July 2008.
18. The United Wa State Party: Narco–Army or Ethnic Nationalist Party? Tom Kramer, East West Center.
19. Bertil Lintner and Michael Black. 'A detailed discussion on the drug trade and production is also given in Merchants of Madness'. *The Sentinel,* 24 June 2008.
20. Anthony Davis. 'Law and Disorder: A Growing Torrent of Guns and Narcotics Overwhelms China'. *Asia Week*, 25 August 1995.
21. Interview with Mrinal Hazarika, former Commandant of ULFA's 28th Battalion, on 2 November 2008; Surya Rangfor, Publicity Secretary of UPDS on 30 January 2007; and James Bond Kuki, Publicity Secretary of UKLF on 19 September 2007.
22. 'NSCN Gun-Runners a Threat to Talks'. *The Times of India*, 26 May 2010.
23. 'Arms Flow Feed Militancy'. *The Telegraph*, Northeast Edition, 29 October 2004. Both Tengchong and Ruili in Yunnan are named as centres where arms are released.
24. Interview with Dilip Nunisa, Chairman of Dima Halam Daogah, 2 April 2008.
25. 'China Emerging as Main Source of Arms to NE Rebels: Janes Review'. *Indian Express*, 22 May 2009.
26. *China Daily,* 9 August 2010, which quotes a report by *Xinhua.*

Note: Many informants, including government officials, militants, and agents involved in selling firearms, requested anonymity.

GOVERNANCE

Human Insecurity in Manipur: A Threat to Humane Governance

K.S. Subramanian

Introduction

A team of concerned citizens including Sumit Chakravartty, Editor, *Mainstream*; Kavita Srivastava, human rights activist and National Secretary of PUCL; Vasundhara Jairath, Delhi Solidarity Group (DSG), and the author visited Imphal from 5 to 10 November 2009 to study the situation resulting from the heightened violence in Manipur during July 2009.

Context

Manipur has been home to sustained conflict and an exceptionally high degree of violence and is today amongst the worst affected states on account of the imposition of the Armed Forces (Special Powers) Act, 1958 (AFSPA). The political situation in this tiny conflict-affected state with a population of 2.6 million in north-east India became explosive after the market shoot-out in Imphal on 23 July 2009 that killed a five-month pregnant woman, Thokchom Rabina Devi, and a young man, Chungkham Sanjit, alleged to be a militant insurgent. Five other persons also suffered injuries in the shoot-out in what is widely

I am grateful to DSG for facilitating this visit and to my team mates for contributing to this case study.

believed to be a fake encounter, though the authorities branded it as an encounter between the alleged insurgent, Sanjit and police commandos. It was due to the people's sustained and intense campaign against the cold-blooded killings that the government eventually suspended the seven police commandos involved in the incident and instituted a one-man Judicial Commission of enquiry headed by a retired judge.

The killings of Sanjit and Rabina evoked people's anger that spilled over to the streets, thereby bringing Manipur in general and Imphal in particular to a halt. This was not a stray incident that just happened in a random shoot-out. According to media reports and human rights activists, Imphal and other hill districts have had about 300 extra-judicial killings in 2009, meaning one such killing every day. People were frustrated that no rule of law existed. The state police was functioning with complete impunity.

Apart from such a large number of extra-judicial killings, hundreds of men and women, including eminent environmental activist Jiten Yumnam, had been picked up and detained under National Security Act (NSA) on the ground that they were allegedly working with or supporting militant groups. The message to the human rights community was very clear: activists and human rights defenders were also targeted and voices of protest would be throttled. The sense of frustration became even more intense as the rest of India and the powers that be in Delhi refused to respond despite bringing the issues to the notice of the Union of India and through the media to the country. The historic non-violent struggle of Irom Sharmila Chanu demanding the repeal of AFSPA that entered its tenth year on 5 November 2009 had become a rallying point for believers in human rights and democracy instilling hope as reflected in the Festival on Justice, Peace and Hope that took place around the same time.

Our main concerns were centred on two key points: (i) examination of allegations of fake killings and illegal detentions in the state by looking at a few cases and (ii) response of the state machinery to these allegations.

The Terms of Reference of our committee were:

i. to visit and interact with families of those killed in alleged fake encounters;
ii. to take account of the number of people killed, arrested, tortured, detained, etc. by security forces;
iii. to interact with those in jail or those released after detention/arrest;
iv. to meet the Chief Minister and other officials concerned with the law and order situation;
v. to prepare a narrative and photo documentation of the visit; and
vi. to compile a comprehensive report of facts collected with analysis and recommendations and present it to all the stakeholders and national/regional media.

Those whom we met include Irom Sharmila Chanu, who has been on an indefinite fast since November 2000 demanding repeal of AFSPA; Okram Ibobi Singh, Chief Minister; Yunman Joykumar Singh, Director-General of Police; Anand Prakash, Inspector General of Prisons, Arms and Operations and Human Rights; families of Sanjit and Rabina; members of the Extrajudicial Executions Victim Families' Association, Manipur (EEVFAM); members of the Joint Action Committees (JACs) of Sanjit and Rabina's killings; family of NSA detainee Jiten Yumnam; retired Sessions Judge C. Upendra who has headed twelve judicial enquiries relating to law and order in Manipur; member of the Manipur Human Rights Commission, Lt Col (retd) R.S. Rajkumar; family of former NSA detainee, Lourembam Nganbi Devi; and senior civil society leaders, academics, and media persons.

The Killing of Chungkham Sanjit on 23 July 2009

Official Version

On the morning of 23 July 2009, a pregnant woman and a young man were killed and five others injured in a shooting incident in the crowded Khwairamband Keithel of Imphal. The Manipur State Assembly was in session. Okram Ibobi Singh, Chief Minister of the State, read out the following statement prepared by the police:

> A suspicious looking youth was asked to stop by a team of Imphal West Police Commandos, while they were on frisking duty, near the Bhagyachandra statue at about 10:30 am. When the youth was asked to stop, he pulled out a gun and fired towards the frisking party. The youth managed to flee along the BT Road. The police party dived and retaliated immediately and chased the fleeing youth, who fired towards the public indiscriminately, in a bid to escape. But the youth was finally cornered inside Maimu Pharmacy at the BT Road. The youth was asked to surrender but instead of surrendering, the youth again opened fire but he was killed in a retaliatory fire.

The Chief Minister further stated that the police could recover one 9 mm pistol (Mauser) loaded with three live rounds in the chamber and one driving license issued in the name of one Chungkham Sanjit, son of Ch. Khelson of Khurai Kongpal Sajor Leikai, Manipur, issued by the Licensing and Registering Authority, Transport Department, Senapati.

L. Kailun, Senior Superintendent of Police (SSP), Imphal West District, Manipur, during his press release that evening not only dished out a similar statement as that of the CM, but went on to argue that Sanjit was a militant with a past record of several cases registered against him and had been arrested earlier. Para 3 of the press release began with the line, 'Chungkham Sanjit alias Ramesh alias Ngongo alias Chingkei (27) was arrested earlier on two occasions under (i) FIR No 245(11) 2000 u/s 10/13 of the UA(P)A Act, Sec 5 Explosives Act and 212 IPC at Porompat Police Station on 27/11/2000 by CDO Imphal East and (ii) FIR number 189(7) 07 u/s 17/20 of UA (P)A

Act of Imphal P.S. on 2/07/2007 by CDO Imphal West. He was also detained under NSA 12 on 19/07/2007 (Democracy "Encountered": Rights' Violations in Manipur) . At the time of his first arrest he was holding the rank of corporal in PLA under army no. 2338'.

Family's Version

The team visited Sanjit's house and met his mother, grandmother, sister, and friends. The family was still in mourning. There was a small plate with a few marigold flowers and a bowl with water lying in the centre of the courtyard, which had a fresh coating of clay. We were told that the ritual would continue for a year. We were also told that Sanjit had been a house painter and the main breadwinner of his family. Apart from painting he also worked in the nights as a care giver (attendant) in Raj Polyclinic hospital. With his earnings through working day and night he looked after the needs of his eleven-member joint family. His father is a mechanic and he had three younger brothers. Vishal, the eldest of the three, sat at some distance from us and looked deeply disturbed.

Chungkham Taratombi Devi, Sanjit's mother, told us:

> I am 45 years old. My son was 23 years. On 23 July morning at about 8:30 am, Sanjit left home for the hospital with food for his uncle, who was admitted in the Medicine ward of the Jawaharlal Nehru Hospital.
>
> At 9:30 am he left the hospital and came to the market place to buy medicines as all the medicines were not available at the hospital store. He travelled by auto and came to BT Road. Sometime later in the morning we received news about the firing in the bazaar. A friend, who stayed behind at the hospital when Sanjit went to the market, got worried when he heard about the firing and tried to locate him. He called him several times on the mobile, but there was no response. His cousin called the family and asked whether they knew about

> his whereabouts. The family also kept calling his number but there was no response. Eventually the phone was answered by someone and there was a very rude reply. His cousin did not understand what was happening. After a while the phone was switched off.
>
> At around 3 pm, some policemen came from Imphal West police station and informed us that Sanjit had been killed in an encounter. They said that Sanjit had refused to be frisked and instead fired indiscriminately at the crowd killing one woman and injuring five others. They first used the loudspeaker asking him to surrender. He, instead, fired back. So the police chased him and retaliated by firing back at him which proved fatal.

All this had been written in the FIR that they filed in the case of Rabina. The police lodged FIR number 75/07/09, u/s 302, 326, 307, 506 IPC, 17/20 UAPA, Sec 1(b) Arms Act. It is a case against Sanjit filed by Herojit Singh, CDO, West Imphal district. Sanjit's mother told us that he had joined the People's Liberation Army (PLA) when he was only 12 years old. He was arrested twice and also detained in jail under NSA. He was released from jail in 2007 when he left the PLA on health grounds. He has also been regularly appearing before the court. Since his conduct was very good the court had even exempted him from appearance. Sanjit's mother said that she would oppose the police story till she breathed her last. He could never have fired at the crowd. She said she never went inside the mortuary. The family refused to take the body for three days; later they did. They had said that they would not take the body till justice was delivered. She said that the local press had been writing that the killing took place in a fake encounter. Tehelka magazine published the photos of the fake encounter in its 8 August issue, which was available on the stands on 1 August. The photos shocked the family as well as others in Manipur. The family lodged an FIR against the police. There were strong agitations and the government on 6 August 2009 suspended the seven commandos who were involved in the incident.

Sanjit's mother said,

> It was a long struggle to get the FIR lodged. We went to the police station on the 7th of August to get the FIR lodged. They refused. We then went to the High Court in Imphal on 17th September. It took time and the High Court directed the police to lodge a case. The government sent feelers to us telling that they would give us ₹ 10 lakh if we did not pursue the case and stopped supporting the movement for justice for Sanjit and Rabina. But we refused to be purchased. We will not give up till justice is meted out. We want justice for Sanjit.

On the Killing of Rabina

In the evening of 6 November, the team members visited the residence of Rabina Devi, who was killed by a stray bullet that pierced through her head. They met Thokchom Chinglensana, her husband, and Russel, her child, along with other family members. Thokchom said he had gone to his mobile shop (where he worked) early in the morning on 23 July.

Rabina was to go for a medical check-up that day. She was five months pregnant. 'I asked her to come to the shop and told her that we would go together to the doctor', Thokchom informed, adding, 'I was in the shop when the firing took place. It was only at 3:30 pm that a friend came and told me about Rabina's death in the firing. My mobile was not working that day, so I could not be informed earlier.' Asked as to who killed her, Thokchom replied, 'I think the (police) commandos did it— the men in khaki'.

It was learnt from Rabina's family that her relatives went to the police to file a complaint. Initially, the police refused to accept the complaint. The next morning they prepared a report and gave it to the Lamsang police station under which their residence falls. They also sent a petition to the Manipur Human Rights Commission (MHRC), which then initiated investigation proceedings. When summoned by the Commission the police declined to make any statement. Thereafter, the government asked MHRC to stop investigation. But MHRC refused. The government then went to the Imphal Bench of the High Court and got a stay. Thockchom further added that to avail of the compensation they had to make an application to the authorities and he was not interested in doing so.

Thokchom was asked whether he would depose before the Judicial Commission set up to inquire into the 23 July incident. He bluntly said, 'I don't believe in the Judicial Commission. I only believe in the Manipur Human Rights Commission.'

Based on local media reports and human rights activists perhaps the events could be traced thus: On 23 July 2009 in the forenoon, the Manipur Police commandos were carrying out frisking operations against suspected terrorists on BT Road. A young man with a firearm was apprehended but he escaped police custody (Democracy 'Encountered': Rights' Violations in Manipur). While chasing him to recover the firearm, the commandos resorted to indiscriminate firing/ or fired carelessly (whichever may be the case). Or perhaps the safety device on one of the firearms was not on. One of the bullets from the automatic weapon carried by a commando hit and killed the 23-year-old pregnant woman, Rabina, and injured five others. The police commandos were discomfited by the unplanned killing and started looking for an appropriate scapegoat. Luckily, they were able to locate former militant Sanjit who was doing some medical shopping for his uncle. They caught hold of Sanjit, dragged him into a nearby pharmacy/watch-repair shop, shot him dead at point blank range and planted a weapon on him to convince the public that he had shot and killed Rabina. Both the bodies were then placed in a truck and taken away. The police thereafter put out the story that Sanjit, the former militant, was the man behind the killing of Rabina. This provoked massive public outcry against the killings. On 1 August photographs published in *Tehelka* magazine told a tale that disproved the police story. Further, the two violent killings by the police commandos and the explanation put out by the authorities did not carry any conviction with the public who disbelieved the official version. There was outrage and protest which led to massive demonstrations on the streets. Nevertheless, at the team's meeting with him, the State DGP maintained that Sanjit was a hardened militant who fired recklessly killing Rabina and that the 'Tehelka' photos were fake!

In the wake of the public outcry against the killings in the middle of the busiest market in the heart of Imphal in broad daylight, a spontaneous people's movement was thrown up supported by several organisations, a day after the killings of Sanjit and Rabina, including Apunba Lup, an umbrella body of over 30 groups spearheading the struggle against AFSPA, joined and supported by students' unions such as All Manipur Students' Union (AMSU), Manipur Students' Federation (MSF), and Kangleipak Students' Association (KSA), along with two joint action committees formed simultaneously.

The following were the demands made by various groups:

i. The Chief Minister (CM) should resign on moral grounds. The CM also happened to hold the home portfolio. He had misinformed the state Assembly on the sequence of events that resulted in the killing of Sanjit. They demanded that if he was not willing to step down as the CM, he must at least step down as the Home Minister.
ii. Suspend top police and administrative officials under whom these killings have taken place, including the DGP, SSP and SP;
iii. Take strict legal action against the police commandos directly involved in the incidents and termination of their services (some groups even demanded that they should be sentenced to life imprisonment);
iv. Return the documents and other materials seized from the office of the member organisations of Apunba Lup;

v. Release the activists arrested during the agitation in this period unconditionally;
vi. Repeal AFSPA;
vii. End the practice of fake encounters.

The two JACs also presented these demands to the Union Home Secretary and other delegations that came from Delhi. They included the parliamentary team of BJP on 18 August; the National United Women's Front on 20 August; the Union Home Secretary on 22 August; and Dr Ramachandran, a CPI (M) MP, on 4 September. A memorandum addressed to the PM was delivered to Union Minister Agatha Sangma on 20 October. They also pursued their demands with the local Congress party leaders in Imphal.

Opposition parties also demanded the dismissal of the Congress-led SPF government headed by Ibobi and the imposition of President's Rule. The government's response was three fold. On 1 August the Additional Secretary (Home) ordered that the District Magistrate (DM) of West Imphal district may carry out a probe of the 23 July killings. The report was to be submitted within 30 days. The notification issued by the DM stated that the enquiry would begin on 4 August in the court room of DM, Imphal West. In this connection the authorities decided to seize all the newspapers published between 24 and 27 July as well as copies of the relevant *Tehelka* issue. It may be added here that since the 2006 amendment of the CrPC, every custodial killing has to be mandatorily investigated by a judicial magistrate. The law of the land does not seem to be applicable in this matter in Manipur as the Executive Magistrate was asked to investigate. When people's pressure through bandhs, marches, and demonstrations continued to rise and did not show any sign of abating, CM announced on 5 August that the members of the Manipur police force responsible for the 23 July incident would be suspended and that a judicial enquiry would be instituted. Subsequently the following actions were taken by the government:

1. Seven police commandos allegedly involved in the killing of Sanjit were suspended on 6 August 2009.

2. Retired Chief Justice of Guwahati High Court Justice P.C. Agarwal agreed on 28 August to conduct a judicial enquiry instituted under the Commissions of Enquiry Act, 1952, to investigate the firing incident and to give suggestions so that such incidents are not repeated.

However, the Government of Manipur refused to respond to the people's demand for justice and an end to arbitrary killings in the state. The government instead arrested several of the agitators between 4 August and 14 September. Up to 26 people were arrested, 10 of them under NSA. Later, provisions of NSA were revoked in the case of six. Four, including Jiten Yumnam, continued to be detained in the Sajiwa Central Jail under NSA. Besides NSA, UAPA was also slapped on eleven activists. While bail has now been granted to most besides the four still in custody under NSA, several of them have refused to accept bail. They demanded withdrawal of the false charges. Amongst those arrested were office bearers of organisations that led the protests, such as Apunba Lup, All Manipur United Clubs Organization (AMUCO), Apunba Manipur Kanba Imma Lup (AMKIL) and Poirei Leimarol Apunba Meira Paibi Lup, the last two being constituent organisations of Apunba Lup.

In early September when the people of Manipur felt that the government was not sincere in responding to the people's call for justice and an end to arbitrary killings, AMSU called for indefinite boycott of classes in schools in the districts of the valley. This was supported by MSF and KSA among other student unions as well as by Apunba Lup. Despite appeals by the Education Minister, the call for indefinite boycott of classes was implemented. This affected about a hundred thousand students. This call was implemented by several schools. Many organisations of parents and other groups, however, appealed to the student bodies and even protested that it would affect the future of students and, therefore, this should be called off while agitating for justice. To break the impasse, talks were held on 31 October between the leaders of the people's movement and the CM and other senior ministers and officials of the government, including police representatives. The members from the public who had been formally invited included coordinators / assistant coordinators of Apunba Lup, Presidents of AMSU, MSF, and KSA along with convenors of the two JACs.

However, little was resolved. The government agreed to transfer the SP of Imphal (West) where the killings took place, to ensure free and fair enquiry. However, he was transferred to Imphal (East), where Sanjit's family lived, and SP, Imphal (East) was transferred to Imphal (West)!

Fake Encounters in Manipur

Official Version

During the team's meetings with official representatives of the state, including CM (on 7 October), DGP (on 6 October) and IG Prisons (on 5 October), it was clear that the state's prime concern was tackling insurgency. The DGP confirmed that over 260 people have been killed since January 2009 and affirmed that all of them were underground militants, activists, or insurgents. Manipur does not recognise any such thing as 'extra-judicial killing' in the state. According to DGP, there had not been a single proven case of this. He said that they had foolproof, hundred per cent evidence that those killed were members of the underground; none of them was innocent. However, his contention did not answer the question as to why they could not instead have been arrested and put under trial. IG Prisons, in the context of combating insurgency in the state, stated, 'When a surgical operation takes place, there must be pain.'

Official sources gave the following information about the security manpower deployed in the state as of 1 November 2009.

Force	Number of personnel
Manipur Rifles (MR) and India Reserve Battalions (IRB)	10,396 (six battalions each)
Various civil police units	5,056
Central Paramilitary Forces (CRPF and BSF)	10, 450
Army	10 battalions (approximately 10,000)
Assam Rifles	26 battalions (approximately 26,000)
Home Guards	2,312

The data on all cases registered and the number of persons/cases in 2008 and 2009 were as follows:

Year	Number of cases registered	Conviction
2008	3349	67 persons in 64 cases
2009 (up to 8 November)	3348	26 persons in 15 cases

It is thus clear that

i. Manipur with a population of only about 2.6 million has too many military and paramilitary forces and too few civilian police forces. This means that the basic purpose of policing, namely, service delivery to the public, is down-graded at the cost of maintenance of order which is prioritised.
ii. The number of cases registered per year (including those related to normal as well as extraordinary crime) is not large and the rate of conviction is poor.

Both features are disturbing. The team members expressed concern that more than a fourth of the prisoners in Manipur were detained under NSA. They particularly mentioned the case of human rights defender Jiten Yumnam. The DGP defended his detention and asserted that he too had connections with the underground militants. In the DGP's view, all forms of public protest that took place in the state came only from armed militant and insurgent groups!

That there exists in the public mind a sense of anger against and strong opposition to the way the government was functioning was simply denied. His logic was based on the assumption that the people of Manipur, being tired of the armed militants, would find no reason to oppose the killing of yet another militant (Sanjit). This statement meant that all those protesting on the streets were cadres of armed militant groups. He also insisted that Apunba Lup was basically a front of armed militant groups.

The same logic was applied in the case of Jiten's active involvement in the public opposition to Tipaimukh dam. The DGP insisted that the dam could not provoke public opposition since there was nothing to oppose – waterways, irrigation, electricity, or security forces. It was thus taken for granted that the protest over Tipaimukh dam (proposed height 160 mts) was because the area where the dam is to be built was allegedly a UNLF stronghold. When asked point blank if this meant that the state sees all those who are opposing Tipaimukh dam today as insurgents, the DGP's response was a simple 'Yes'.

It is also worth mentioning here that while the DGP drew such a connection between Jiten's involvement in resistance to the Tipaimukh dam and UNLF, the FIR lodged by the police against Jiten accuses him of links with PLA. It also happens that UNLF and PLA, both proscribed groups, are rival insurgent groups in Manipur.

On the matter of prisoners in Manipur prisons, the officer in charge who also holds charges of IG Human Rights, Home Guards Training, and IG Arms and Operations, in response to a query as to why were there such large numbers of prisoners in Manipur's jails, particularly those detained under NSA, stated 'We have a capacity of 900 in our jails and there are only 600 prisoners. We want 300 more to fill the vacancy'. On the agitation led by Apunba Lup against the 23

July incident, both the CM and the DGP claimed that Apunba Lup was nothing but a front organisation of insurgent groups. Student unions such as AMSU, MSF, and KSA were also claimed to be false student unions and front organisations of armed insurgent groups. The photographs published by *Tehelka* and reproduced by local media were also claimed by the DGP to have been 'doctored'. He further refuted the post-mortem report of Rabina that revealed that she was killed by a long range rifle (and not by a 9 mm pistol that Sanjit allegedly possessed), stating that the concerned doctor did not know his duty and it was none of his business to speak of what firearm was used in the killing!

All said and done, the CM did say that he was ready for a second round of talks with the agitating groups. The first round was held on 31 October, but few issues were resolved. However, he also underlined the fact that several of their demands such as repeal of AFSPA; resignation of CM on moral grounds; removal of several top officials like the DGP; termination of services of the seven commandos suspended after the 23 July incidents, and sentencing them to life imprisonment, could never be met.

As regards AFSPA, CM disclosed that it had been lifted from seven assembly constituencies in Imphal. But the decision of its repeal could be taken only by the Centre. He informed that while the Nagaland government attempted to withdraw AFSPA from certain areas the Central Government opposed this move twice. The DGP also stated that while all operations against militant Kuki groups have been suspended and Naga groups are observing a ceasefire, the valley groups are yet to come to the table for talks. He, however, also said that they were in a dialogue with the Centre regarding fencing the Indo–Myanmar border on the Manipur side and deployment of troops. Anand Prakash, IG Prison and Human Rights, asked why social activists do not agitate when non-Manipuris are attacked. According to him, several attacks had taken place on non-Manipuris by suspected militant groups. Since 1 November in separate incidents two Biharis were killed, a scavenger and a butcher. They were fired at from point blank range. One was shot in the forehead.

According to Prakash, a possible explanation is that they could be retaliatory killings following an ambush by Assam Rifles on 30 October where seven alleged militants were killed. He, however, added that this was a mere speculation and needed to be probed further as no armed group has claimed responsibility for these incidents. He also stated that the underground leaders were extortionists and could kill anybody under a contract. He alleged that they killed Prof. Islamuddin in the University of Manipur campus. (We learnt from other sources that one of those involved in the murder of Prof. Islamuddin was a personnel of IRB. He has been detained under NSA. The matter has been handed over to CBI for enquiry.) Also, an SDPO was brutally murdered last year. He also stated that the Government of Manipur, as part of preventing cash from being diverted to militants, had completed the first phase of putting in place the system of transfer of all salaries through banks. In Manipur, 97 per cent employees have bank accounts. In the second phase, payments to all the work of contractors and to other programmes, including those under National Rural Employment Guarantee Scheme (NREGS), were to be carried out through banks. He felt that this would make a difference.

Victims' Families' Version

We met more than 12 women whose husbands or sons had been killed in encounters in the last few years. These women formed the Extrajudicial Executions Victim Families' Association, Manipur (EEVFAM). They meet regularly to pursue their common battle with the state. Most of the wives belonged to the age group of 20 to 35 with small children. Some mothers also came and shared their woes and struggles. All of them broke down when they shared their stories. The loss of their husbands and sons, often the main breadwinner, has left them shattered. No FIRs were lodged in any of the cases and no compensation paid. They have also to live with the stigma of being the wife or mother of a terrorist.

Some distinctive features in the so-called encounters were isolated locations, absence of casualties of security forces; recovery of 9 mm pistols or hand grenades in most cases; combination of force of the police commandos units and central security forces; the victim being taken away from home or elsewhere and killed at another place; removal of money, mobile phones and other valuables from the victims; and so on.

After the killings

- No NHRC guidelines are followed.
- No magisterial enquiry takes place under section 175 of CrPC.
- Post-mortem reports are never provided to the families if at all they take place. Video recording is done only on written requests.
- No inquest takes place at the site of the incident.
- No FIR gets lodged when relatives want the deaths investigated.
- If NHRC or the High Court intervenes, then the state government keeps the cases pending for years.
- No rehabilitation of the families of the victims ever takes place.

During these meetings many of the women broke down when they spoke. They were still coping with raw wounds keenly awaiting the delivery of justice. All of them believe that their husbands had been wrongfully killed. But it was even worse that they had been left to look after the children and old parents with no support from the government.

Renu Hangzo, 28 years, President of EEVFAM, told us of her husband's death:

> On 6 April 2007, my husband, along with two of his friends, was returning from the market on a scooter. A team of police commandos were frisking passersby at Kwakeithel, about 1 km from our house. Apparently, they had been asked to

> stop but they might not have heard the police as there were many others being stopped. Within a short time, the police commandos reportedly chased them by firing at them. Mr Paka, the pillion rider, was hit at the back. As a result, the scooter skidded and they fell on the road. The two of them, including my husband, were still alive. Immediately, the police surrounded the two pointing their guns at them. Thereafter, they were asked to remove their shirt and made to sit and then stand up while raising their hands. All the while the police were laughing and threatening them. The scene was witnessed by the local people who were trying to help them. Since the police fired at witnesses, they were not allowed to intervene. Both of them were brutally and mercilessly subjected to torture. They were then shot at point blank range on the forehead and inside the mouth.[1]

No action was taken against the killers. But she still awaits justice in her case and that of other women. A magisterial enquiry was conducted into the incident. The report was, however, not made public.

Edina, 29 years, General Secretary of the Association, told us that on 21 January 2009 her 31-year-old husband left for work on his scooter at 10:30 am. At 3 pm the police picked him up from in front of the DM College in Imphal and took to Makhal village in Senapati district in a white Gypsy. The police insisted that he belonged to the outlawed organisation called KYKL. He never returned. He was the main breadwinner of the family and was an auto driver. He is survived by his wife, 7-year-old son, 4-year-old daughter, and his mother with a heart disease. When Edina tried to file an FIR at Porompat police station in Imphal (East), they did not lodge it. She struggled and got an NHRC enquiry instituted. NHRC asked the home department to look into the allegations. Nothing has come out of this.

According to Ranjita, 25 years, her husband Satish Loithongbom was picked up on 16 May and killed on 18 May. Her husband and his friend had gone to Sajiwa jail to meet his brother who had been arrested in a case relating to a builder. According to eyewitnesses, when they were on their way back from jail, they were picked up by five police personnel in a gypsy and handed over to the Assam Rifles (AR). On 18 May the friend was released and handed over to Manipur Police by AR. Satish was taken to Laikot hills in Imphal (East) and killed. When an MLA raised this issue in the state Assembly, the CM reportedly asked him if he was an eyewitness to the incident! The family moved the Guwahati High Court. Two of the police commandos were suspended. According to the affidavit filed by Assam Rifles, the encounter took place in Laikot hills.

Mumtaz told us that her husband Azad, a college lecturer who was planning to pursue his Ph.D., was killed on 7 March 2009 in Dimapur transit camp. Azad used to teach Chemistry in Waikhon Mani Girls College in Imphal. He, along with another boy, had been picked up earlier by AR and charged with carrying illegal weapons and jailed. He was granted bail on health grounds. He moved to Delhi as he was keen to pursue his Ph.D. She also met him at Guwahati and handed over his documents. She thought he would do his Ph.D. from Siliguri. However, she last heard from him on 2 March when he told her he was going to be involved in talks with People's United Liberation Front (PULF) (a largely Muslim self-determination group in Manipur), as a local elderly, for the suspension of operations. Mumtaz mentioned she was not happy with her husband's decision to get involved and pleaded with him not to go ahead with this. On 6 March the agreement on suspension of operations was to be signed and declared in Delhi on 15 March. On 6 March he was at the army transit camp in Dimapur and on the 7th he was killed along with three others including a young boy. No FIR had been lodged in this case. Mumtaz also did not have a death certificate and no document to show that her husband had been killed in a false encounter.

Sanaa's husband Iboyaima, a businessman, was killed on 1 July 2008 in a false encounter. Her husband was carrying 3.5 lakh rupees when he was picked up and killed by the police. There were huge protests by their community when the news of his killing reached them. However, no FIR could be lodged and no inquest took place. She is in a very vulnerable situation even today as she has no support.

According to Neena, Treasurer of the Association, on 4 November 2008 her husband Michael (34 years) had gone out with a friend after lunch. After some time he called them and said that he had been arrested. He also did not know why he had been arrested. She said that after that she could not speak to him. They rushed to the close by police station but he was not there. It was only later that they saw the body of her husband with a hand grenade on ISTV. The Imphal (West) police gave out the story of an encounter. The encounter happened in the Lamsang police station area. Her family members went and met the local Meira Paibi women who said that there was no encounter. Her husband was said to have been caught from Wahengbam Leikai. She believes that he was killed as he had invested in some capital projects and he was killed by the Manipur police commandos for money. No FIR had been filed and no case had been lodged with the NHRC.

Chandrakala informed us that her 24-year-old son Priyobrata of Mangsangei Bonoimakhong village was killed on 15 March at the Longol Game village. He had gone out of the house on his bike with ₹8,000 to buy a camera. The police killed him for the money and claimed that he was a member of the underground Kangleipak Communist Party (KCP) and was killed in retaliatory fire. Chandrakala vehemently denies this. She said she was informed of his murder on the 16th. She refused to take the body for eight days. The local MLA then convinced her to take the body which she did subsequently. She, however, never got back his belongings or his bike.

Sakhi lost her son, Somendro, who had gone out to get some money from the home of his girlfriend whom he was to marry shortly. Even before he reached her house he had been killed. It is from ISTV that they learnt about his death. He used to run a hotel. Here also they feel that he had been killed by the commandos for money. The police claimed that he was killed in an encounter.

According to Sanjukta, on 29 March her husband, like any other day, went to work on his scooter. On his way back he was trailed by two armed men in civil dress on a scooter. It was later learnt that they were policemen. They shot him dead in front of his mother in his own courtyard. They did not take back the body for 10 days. NHRC directed the state government to conduct a magisterial enquiry. She was not sure as to what had happened to it. They had received no summons to depose.

On rehabilitation of families of those killed, CM and DGP told us that a rehabilitation centre was being set up 70 km away from Imphal where 100 acres of land had been acquired. We told them that the rehabilitation had to be at multiple levels and these women would face a situation of displacement if they were sent hundreds of kilometres away. This would also result in losing the support of their families which was essential in such a situation. We tried to press on the CM that rehabilitation should consist of guarantee of lifelong education for the children, a pension-like cash guarantee scheme for the parents, and a job for the wife. The CM said that other than the rehabilitation centre no scheme was planned. The DGP added that if a person was killed then an ex-gratia payment was made to the survivors. However, the family had to make an application.

They said that Rabina's family deserved it but they were not interested in taking it as they were under the influencc of the Apunba Lup.

Meeting with Manipur Human Rights Commission

Lt Col (retd) R.S. Rajkumar, Member of the Manipur Human Rights Commission, told the team that after the 23 July incident, he took the statements of 31 people including those injured in the incident. He added in his interim report that Rabina's post-mortem report had clearly indicated that she was killed due to rifle injury from a distance whereas 'the cause of death of Ch. Sanjit Meitei was due to the firing from short-range firearm, like a pistol'. He further mentioned in his interim report that 'there was no evidence of cross-firing. ... Therefore, the statements of the police witnesses are urgently necessary. ... The police witnesses should give statements for their own defence. ... Absence without any response will go against them.' However, the police did not respond. We also learnt that the government of Manipur sought a stay on the MHRC enquiry in view of the setting up of a judicial commission.

Fake Encounters, Police Recruitment, and Culture of Impunity

1. The Manipur police force has been awarded with a large number of awards by the Government of India. Of the total of 220 gallantry awards given away by the President of India, 74 were given to Manipur Police.
2. Some of those policemen who have been implicated in the killings of Sanjit and Rabina have also received the President's medals. We do not know what citations were made to give the award.
3. Recruitments to the Manipur police reportedly depend on a minimum bribe of ₹ 2 lakh for constables and ₹ 12 lakh for ASIs.
4. Head Constable Herojit Singh, who lodged the FIR after the murders of Rabina and Sanjit, and was later suspended in the wake of public outcry, has reportedly killed more than 80 people in the name of counter-insurgency operations and yet roams freely without any charges!
5. We were told that several cases of sexual violence by the police have been reported.
6. AFSPA has created a culture of impunity for all security forces. Although the Manipur Police force are accountable to the law, the prevailing culture of impunity affects them as well since AFSPA has been in force in the Manipur valley ever since 1980 and in

the hills even longer. This has made the Manipur Police trigger happy. We were informed that the culture of impunity was legal, socio-political, and even cultural.

7. We were told that in West and East Imphal districts AFSPA did not apply. Still Manipur commando forces often inflicted violence on innocents here.
8. A retired senior police officer informed us that the police force was deficient in training. Manipur Police did not yet have a new Police Act as recommended by the Supreme Court in the Prakash Singh case. He added that recruitment to the police force is a big money-spinner and recruitment continued constantly while there was complete ban on recruitment to all other departments.

Judicial Enquiries in Manipur

After talking to a cross-section of people who were agitating against fake encounters in Manipur, a few broad points emerged. These fake encounters take place regularly. The demand of the protestors has been to investigate the cases and punish the guilty. However, the government has not made even a single report of judicial enquiries public. That is why there is a general scepticism and little faith in these enquiries. Retired Sessions Judge C. Upendra told us that he had headed twelve such enquiries himself, and found that in all cases the encounters were fake, though none of his reports was made public. MHRC has also been made dysfunctional. In the case of the 23 July killings, the police refused to depose before MHRC and the commission was ordered by the state government to end its enquiry. MHRC's enquiry has been stayed by the High court. A final decision is still pending with the court.

On 27 August 2009 the state government issued a notification vide order No. 2/1(81)/2009-H constituting a one-man Judicial Commission of Enquiry headed by Justice (retd) P.G. Agarwal of the Guwahati High Court to inquire into the incident with the following two terms of reference:

a. Fact and circumstances leading to the incident of firing and death of Smt. Thokchom Rabina Devi (23) w/o Th. Chinglensana Singh (24) of Lamshang Bazar, Lamdeng Khunou and Shri Chungkham Sanjit Meitei (22) s/o Ch. Khelen Meitei of Khurai Sajor Leikai and bullet injury to five others viz. (i) Smt Wangkheirakpam Gitarani Devi (40) w/o (L) W. Nongyai @ Nongyaijao Singh d/o Ningthoukhongjam Nobin Singh of Tendongyang, (ii) Golmei Mangal Rongmei (59) s/o G. Lemba Rongmei of Mahakabui Nameihing Keithelmanbi, New Cachar Rd, (iii) Ningthoujam Kishorani Devi (43) w/o N. Raghumani Singh of Narankonjin, (iv) Pangambam Lukhoi Singh (30) s/o (L) P. Pakchao Singh of Heingang Makha Leikai, and (v) Kangabam Subhachandra Singh (40) s/o K. Shamungou Singh of Kha Potsangbam.
b. Recommendation to prevent recurrence of such incidents in future.

C. Upendra told us about two points contained in the previous judicial enquiries—whether the killing was avoidable, and who were responsible for it—were missing in these terms of reference.

Meeting with Irom Sharmila

On 6 November the team had the opportunity to meet with Irom Sharmila Chanu, now on the thirteenth year of her heroic fast demanding repeal of AFSPA. Being allowed to have only a limited number of visitors, she expressed her desire to meet, and speak to more people more often. Her strength and courage in undertaking the longest satyagraha in the world, completely peaceful and non-violent, left the team members in awe of her struggle. She expressed her anguish over the situation in Manipur. In a message during the meeting she said:

> When will we get back our human rights? The government asks why we are making such a hue and cry over the death

> of one or a few. But we need to ponder over how the deaths occurred – by a disease or by the pangs of separation of our beloved … we need to think ... Do we have anything to feel proud of while surviving in this land? Everywhere you see emptiness and hollowness and subjugation. Are we made so differently by god that we as humans do not deserve justice? My heart pains as a human.

It is necessary to mention here a comment made by IG Prisons when asked about Irom Sharmila and her mode of resistance. While he chose not to comment on her struggle he made an insensitive remark relating to the expenses the government was incurring to 'nurse' Sharmila – '9,000–10,000 per month on nose feeding alone, besides several dedicated staff (nurses), to constantly monitor her condition. Added to this were several security personnel.'

Since Mahashweta Devi was denied permission to meet her the previous day, Sharmila handed over a letter for the respected Magsaysay Award winner.

Major Findings

- Huge gap exists between the official version, the victims' families' version, and public opinion in Manipur on alleged encounters in general and on the 23 July incident in particular. In order for democracy to sustain in the light of the massive public protests, the government must necessarily investigate each one of these questionable killings.
- The precedent set by the government of Manipur has been to engage the public in magisterial (judicial or executive) enquiries or commissions of enquiry, reports of none of which has ever been made public. This has shattered people's faith in such processes.
- The 2006 Amendment of Section 176 of CrPC provides for mandatory judicial enquiries in all incidences of custodial deaths and rapes. (In most cases studied by us the victim was picked up

from one place and shown to have been killed in another implying custodial killing.) This Section is being completely violated in the state. This Section was not implemented in any of the killings that happened in 2009. This Amendment has brought in transparency to the entire part on evidence in an investigation and it mandates the kin of the victim to get a report.

- The ease with which the Manipur government at the highest level confirmed that more than 260 people were killed in encounters in 2009 in the state and that they were all insurgents implied that killing an insurgent was justified under all circumstances. It also implied that rather than being a law-enforcing agency, the police was acting as an executioner without following the due process of law. For argument's sake if one accepts that all those killed were insurgents, even then there is no reason why the normal legal procedure should not be followed instead of killing them outright.
- Manipur today should be a cause for great deal of anxiety to the people of India, a constitutional democratic republic, since democracy in the state is at a discount. Additionally the alienation of the people from the state seems almost complete. In this connection the Government of India appears to be as much indifferent as the government of Manipur to the agony of the people.
- The official version on the killings, that goes on reasserting itself irrespective of public outcry; the absence of legal action against those responsible for the cold-blooded murders, and the imposition of AFSPA which grants legal immunity to the armed forces, has bred a culture of impunity that has percolated right down to the state police force. While the Manipur police enjoys no legal immunity, the complete absence of the rule of law in the state, as an extended consequence of the imposition of a draconian law like AFSPA for over 25 years in the valley and for over four decades in the hills and the protection granted to it by the state, have given it a high degree of impunity.

- It is worth mentioning here that AFSPA was not in force where the 23 July killings took place—in Khwairamband market of Imphal. Following the rape and murder of Thangjam Manorama by Assam Rifles personnel in 2004, AFSPA was lifted from seven assembly seats in Imphal. More importantly, the Manipur police commandos are a part of the state police force and are not covered by immunity offered by AFSPA. Such a degree of impunity has resulted in the alienation of the citizens of Manipur from the state. As a result of a conspiracy of circumstances these citizens have been caught in a cross-fire and the state's approach has been increasing this sense of alienation.
- The ratio of security forces to civilians is exceptionally high in Manipur. For a population of 2.6 million there are more than 64,000 security personnel in the state (2009 estimate), approximately one security personnel for every 40 civilians!
- In a situation where the government in Manipur traces all forms of peaceful public protests to armed insurgent groups, the call for dialogue with agitationists is rendered meaningless. By its behaviour and actions reflected in its refusal to accept the people's voices of protest and even the existence of a democratic Opposition, the state ensures that there is no space for democratic forms of articulation of people's desires in the state. Laws like the National Security Act (NSA) and the Unlawful Activities (Prevention) Act (UAPA), which deny the basic human rights guaranteed under the Constitution and open up avenues for misuse of arbitrary powers, have been repeatedly applied to smother citizens' aspirations, engendering a stifling atmosphere. Such an environment can only reinforce the prevailing insurgency and armed militancy.
- There is strong public perception of a high degree of corruption in the police force of Manipur. This is buttressed by the large number of gallantry awards (reportedly 74 out of 220 in the country) won by the Manipur Police personnel this year. This is alleged to be

a kind of material incentive to the extra-judicial measures being allowed to be taken by the guardians of law and order.

- There is apparently a complete breakdown in the rule of law. Instead of arresting those claimed to be insurgents and following such procedures as shooting without the intent to kill, the state security forces resort to indiscriminate killing, protected as they are by extraordinary powers derived from Manipur's 'disturbed area' status. The restoration of peace and order must go hand in hand with the promotion of rule of law and justice for the sustenance of democracy. While the state highlights the importance of national security even as a substantial number of people continue to assert the demand for self-determination, the high degree of violence, breakdown of the rule of law, and the climate of impunity have together resulted in a vicious circle with multiple actors (State and non-State) capitalising on the existing lawlessness for furthering their own vested interests, which have no relations with either national security, safety of citizens, or the political right to self-determination.
- This situation breeds a sense of fear psychosis among the citizens and security forces alike, thereby aggravating instability and frustrating the efforts at normalisation for a return to peace, justice and stability.

Recommendations

- Repeal AFSPA.
- Ensure the rule of law.
- Conduct transparent and thorough probe into each one of the alleged fake encounters. Strictly enforce the procedural guidelines issued by NHRC with regard to 'encounters' such as (a) treat every such death as a cognisable offence and take immediate steps to investigate the circumstances leading to the death and (b) as the police themselves are involved, entrust the investigation to an independent agency. Enforce the 2006 Amendment to the CrPC.

- Make public the reports of all magisterial (judicial or executive) enquiries and commissions of enquiry set up to investigate incidents of fake encounters.
- Take action against those found guilty.
- Revoke NSA and withdraw false charges slapped on those demanding justice for Sanjit and Rabina as well as those fighting for democratic rights.
- End all intimidation of those resorting to peaceful and democratic forms of protest and engage in meaningful dialogue to address their concerns, redress their grievances and resolve outstanding problems.
- Immediately bring a halt to all fake encounters.
- Withdraw paramilitary forces from Manipur University campus.
- Provide a just rehabilitation for the families of the deceased and injured.
- Hold the Ibobi Singh government accountable for the deteriorating situation in the state.
- End Irom Sharmila's custody and restore her civil liberties.

Note

1. From Renu's written testimonial

Grassroots Corruption and Governance: The Assam Scenario

Sunil Kaul

The truth must be told. I fail to suggest any correctional systems in Assam despite all analyses of the situation that I try to do. In fact, I feel that common people have understood that an analysis may paralyse them. They have, therefore, learnt either to ignore the situation, or worse, become part of it. I am not surc if what I have seen in the past 15 years of my association with Assam is peculiar to this state or similar to what the rest of India has also seen. Poor governance in most sectors does not help us to understand where maladministration ends and corruption starts. The beauty of corruption is that one can almost never prove it since it leaves no paper trails. Almost everyone on the corrupt side benefits by hiding corruption. So a conspiracy or collusion is always in the making. Instead of giving numbers and figures, I would share some stories from my recent experience.

Government Officials: Ignorant of Laws or Collusive?

You may have heard of the Minimum Wage Act. The website of the Government of Assam shows the unskilled wage labour to be at ₹108 per day or ₹3240 per month. But does that apply to the government itself? Seventy five per cent of the personnel in my local district office get only ₹2500 per month. And mind you, most of these are educated people and they handle paperwork of the bureaucracy. Surprisingly, lecturers in government colleges at salaries of ₹1500 per month for several years are unwilling to speak up lest they may lose the chance to get their job regularised!

The Provident Fund Act is so stringent that even if twenty labourers are employed for even a single day in a month, the employer is supposed to deduct Provident Fund (PF) and deposit it with the authorities, for the employee's security. The government is supposed to ensure that every single employer under its jurisdiction obeys the law. But in reality thousands of government employees have been denied PF benefits for years. Teachers with the Sarva Shiksha Abhiyan (SSA), health workers with National Rural Health Mission (NRHM); forest guards in sanctuaries; clerks in the Deputy Commissioner's (DC's) office; or anyone in a contractual post gets no PF benefits. 'Shutting up' runs like an epidemic that has engulfed us all. The fear of the 'only legitimised goondas aka police' comes first. Fear of the militants and some youth organisations comes second. Some may argue that the power of the police has only increased and reached these levels thanks to the insurgency in the region. Any encounter with the central security organisations like the army and paramilitary forces is similar. We do not know which party may come to know of our conversations. So, in such an AFSPA-ridden environment, all of us in the North-East have learnt to shut up! Consequently, truth has been the biggest casualty. Even if there are people who occasionally challenge the army or the police, they tend to get so selective in their courage that they forget to challenge the 'armed revolutionaries' who too terrorise the people.

Whose Police?

A few years ago, a DIG of Police came to my rural campus. He asked if we needed any help. I work with a voluntary organisation, and ordinarily need a lot of help but experience had taught us not to say 'yes'. I found myself saying 'What help may I get from the police when they themselves do not believe in law?' The DIG needed an explanation for my opinion. I said that I had never seen traffic policemen wearing helmets while riding, so I least expected them to enforce traffic rules. 'Why do you judge us by how we follow law ourselves? We are not paid for that. We are paid to ensure that others follow law!' Many people come to us with problems. I ask them why they did not go to the police. The most common response I get is, 'We are poor people and do not have that kind of money'.

When we were new to the region, one of my colleagues wished to hold a national youth project camp where he planned to call the veteran Gandhian Shri Subba Rao. It required a considerable sum of money to get some 50 youth together and hold the five-day camp to instil the values of manual labour, hard work, and national integration. A committee was set up which included local leaders and officials to raise resources. As is almost the unwritten rule, the DC of the district was made the Chief Patron. The poor DC wrote letters and shouted on the phone, to many a person to donate money for the worthy cause. But his efforts were clearly not enough. His assistant would often call my colleague organising the camp and hand over to him some bundles of notes. Sometimes 10,000; sometimes 20,000. I wondered as to where the money came from, as we never had to sign a receipt. The suspicion was confirmed two days before the camp when panic buttons were pressed because the money was clearly insufficient for the event. The DC was deep in thought trying to think of ways to harness resources. 'Sir, shall I go to Srirampur Gate (the entry into Kokrajhar district in Assam from West Bengal, known for informal 'tax' collections from every truck that passes through) to collect some money?' asked a young man involved with the arrangements. I may have been scandalised at his suggestion but the DC left him far behind by his reply, 'No, you will not be able to get enough. Instead, I will ring the Superintendent of Police (SP) of Kokrajhar district to get the money for you. You just go and collect the money from him!'

Prevention of Terrorism Act (POTA) is often used to hound innocent people. But I have never seen it being used to arrest arrogant and corrupt government officials!

Rural Development Agency

As Advisor to the Commissioners in the PIL on the Right to Food case set up by the Supreme Court, I was asked to convene a joint court of enquiry (JCE) in Morigaon district of Assam to inquire into allegations levelled by a group of villagers led by a young and persistent man named Prafulla Das. The complaint had been sent to every possible authority in Assam. Not surprisingly, the authorities found his charges baseless. Despite siren-blaring convoys of cars—thanks to the DC, and later on his behalf the project director (PD) of District Rural Development Agency (DRDA) being members of the JCE—taking us to this village in Morigaon district, west of Guwahati, people held their ground and reiterated that the complaints were true. Mind you, the complaint was against DRDA headed by the DC as Chairman and the PD as Director. And they had been given to us as members of the enquiry commission! As the enquiry progressed, we had very little to scratch to arrive at our findings. People held out to their complaints in open meetings and refused to be cowed down by the authoritarianism of the officialdom. The cash book shown to us started with a date coinciding with that of the order for the setting up of the JCE must have been received in the Dispur HQs, that is, a few days before they issued the orders on appointment of members. When I demanded to see the last balance of the previous cash book, I was told that the previous accountant had never handed over the cash book!

People in the public hearing on Swarnajayanti Gramin Rozgar Yojana (SGRY), precursor to NREGS, in that village in Morigaon asked to see a muster roll. 'Sir, we keep reading about muster roll in the newspapers. You too were mentioning it sometime ago. None of us has ever seen it. Can you fulfil this wish of ours'? Since the officials in the meeting had conveniently forgotten to carry any, I sent the official car to get a muster roll. An hour later the person came back empty-handed, saying that he had understood that only the muster roll of that particular enquiry was required and that he had left it at his hometown a few hours away and hence he could not get it! He was determined not to allow the people ever to see a muster roll!

We were determined that we would not leave until we had checked this out thoroughly. The next day, we were shown the muster rolls and measurement books all correctly filled up. We did a double check on them by asking for their issue register. We found out that they had been issued just the previous night! In my fifteen years of service, I have travelled a lot and very often to villages. I have asked many poor people who have worked on government projects if they had to sign anywhere after the work. I have never found any person who had ever signed any paper, even while collecting the money in times when cash payment was still being made!

Funnily, the 'perfect' muster roll put up in front of us on the day, also made us laugh for the disingenuousness—40 people for almost 40 days had the same finger impression, probably not even a thumb impression. And it was a dead giveaway because the finger had a clear linear scar right in its middle in every impression! We clearly knew that the junior engineer (JE) in whose charge this muster roll had been would be the 'fall guy' and that his job would be the first and only one to go when we file our report. But we added something more to the report.

We reported what a senior officer of the district told us on the last day. It was his 'wish to let us know the entire truth'. As the enquiry was not against him, he could easily tell us that the rot started right from the top. But he insisted that we should not cite his name as he would then deny what he had told us.

What he told us was shocking. He said that a fixed amount of money, ₹ 26 crore if my memory serves, was to be deposited by every PD, DRDA of a district into a call deposit account in the State Bank of India (SBI). That was one of the main reasons why there was no way one could control the bungling as papers had to be fudged. In fact, he even said that in his previous posting at Dispur he often used to be sent with bribes to the Centre to ensure delay in the release of money, ostensibly to enable a blame-free heist. The call deposit story was confirmed from other government officials. But it seems that the modus operandi has changed. Maybe the new RTI Act has forced a change that is even worse. Much of the cash that is made surplus because of fake muster rolls is ostensibly kept in the BDO's personal bank account to avoid an RTI enquiry!

We hoped that our report would reach the Supreme Court sometime. We thought that an enquiry with such a lead could unravel everything and all of us civil society members agreed and signed on it in the report. The DC, however, signed selectively on some findings and on statements like the one above, he just wrote, 'beyond the purview of the enquiry'. The SC Commissioners shared the report with the state government for it to take action. When no action was reported, many months after the SC Commissioners sent a reminder. Guess what? They showed that the JE had been 'suspended' just as we had predicted, and the previous PD, who we had indicted in our report for having tampered with documents and falsely denying Prafulla Das' allegations when there was enough evidence, had been served a show cause notice. It would have made us happy, had we not noticed that the date of this action was just one day prior to the explanation that they had given in response to the SC Commissioner's reminder!

To complete what appears like a joke, there was a departmental enquiry on the matter to which I was summoned at short notices and I could not attend for some time. Once I even got the summons after the date was over. However, finally I did reach the venue on the appointed time and date. After much waste of time and travel, there was no sign of the investigating officers. I handed over my written statement and returned. It is certain that no action must have been taken. Even the SC Commissioners have given up sending reminders!

When I was working with another NGO in Assam, there were some stray allegations against us when some people thought we had made money on some DRDA scheme. We had, however, never received a single rupee from DRDA. We tried to declare our honesty by asking the DRDA to certify that it had not given any money to us. Ironical, because almost all of us know how corrupt the DRDA itself is.

There is another story regarding DRDA. This story belongs to a district where everyone tried to tell me how honest the PD of the DRDA is. An NGO was trying to get some people their rightful NREGS job cards and bank accounts to get their money as and when they got jobs. NREGA, passed a few years ago, entitles every rural household in India to get at least 100 days of wage labour every year. The PD also sent a letter asking the VCDCs—the equivalent of a Panchayat in some Sixth Schedule areas—to hand over NREGS job cards and bank pass books but to no avail.

To cut a long story short, people in one of these VCDCs came to know through the Internet that while they were being told that there was no scheme to give them employment, money had been showed to have been paid to them through bogus muster rolls. They hauled up the VCDC members and threatened action in case they were not handed over their pass books and job cards. But to their, and to the NGO's, horror, when they got the two even before the deadline, they discovered that all along money had been paid into their bank accounts in the town 50 km away and had also been withdrawn the same day! All that these people had done was to give their photographs for their bank account. They had not even signed any documents to open a bank account. Collectively with the students' unions of the area, the NGO decided to have a public hearing in November, a month after the scandal broke out.

Some surrendered militants in the area, who we learnt had been handed over the job cards, as a way to keep them busy or to eke out a living, were very upset as they were likely to get fixed as most of the allegations pertained to the period when they had the job cards in their custody. They not only threatened people from going to the public hearing but also blocked all the lanes leading to the venue from various villages. Later they even burnt the motor cycle of one of our activists. The enquiry, where more than 40 people came to testify, brought out bizarre stories of job cards having the names of children, often disabled too, all having shown to have worked. Instances were recorded where the same person was shown working on the same day as two individuals, one in his official name and the other in his unofficial name! But in all cases, the basic fact was that they had never been given work when they had asked for, and that they had never known about any deposit or withdrawal of money from their bank accounts. In fact the stories were so stark that even the PD had no choice but to announce a formal government enquiry after a week and also assured that there would be no choice but to lodge FIRs in the case.

After several months of inaction, another enquiry was instituted, thanks to a complaint to the bank ombudsman in Guwahati. Still no action against anyone was reported to have been taken. No one in the region has had the guts to find out why no action was taken as the government—bureaucracy–bank–militant links are crazy like hell! And all this in a district where the PD of the DRDA is considered to be honest and helpful!

Each DRDA has increased its budget exponentially in view of NREGS. While every single poor rural person is expected to get her or his payment made into a bank account that is often 30 to 60 km away, most of the other transactions with contractors and the rest running into lakhs of rupees are almost always paid in cash. I have personally read many auditors blaming this loophole for the poor accounting, but who will prevent the milch cow from being milked?

While one should not expect bank staff to cross-verify all thumb impressions as it is one of the most difficult things to do, one expects them to follow RBI guidelines of keeping a photograph attached to the passbook and account ledger and verifying the poor person by his face. But this difficulty can be made into an opportunity when the administration officials collude with the bank officials. A friend of mine working on forest issues for the past two decades or more told me the following story.

A minister visited his eco-tourist camp and asked him if he needed any help. Since they wanted to upgrade the toilet facilities in the camp they asked for a princely sum of ₹75,000. The minister asked his lackeys to allocate ₹100,000 to his organisation. A few months later, he was called and given ₹90,000 but was asked to sign a receipt for ₹100,000. He was told that the rest was cut for *cha-paanikhoros* (expenses on tea, etc.). When he refused to accept, he was made to sign a receipt for ₹90,000. No sooner had he handed over the money to the villagers to build the toilet than the militants arrived on the scene asking for their share. He and the villagers pleaded that it was too small an amount to be levied a commission. But they would not listen and asked them not to bluff. When the NGO showed their records of having received only ₹90,000, the militants apparently showed them a copy of the actual project grant in their name of almost ten times the amount!

This story, corroborated by other NGOs, who also avail of government grants regularly, shows another modus operandi where bank officials and others collude. The copies of the registration and audits of the NGO ostensibly taken for the small grant are actually used to open an account in the name of the NGO in a small branch, and the officials pocket most of the central government grant allotted to the NGO. They throw some coppers at the NGO so that in case a rare official from Delhi dares to travel to the interiors, they will have something to show!

Another incident that took place last year goes like this. One fine day at around 7 o'clock in the morning we were told that a minister was coming to see our weaving centre. He had already started from a town an hour away. No one knew if it was a central or state minister.

Soon, a cavalcade of cars came. A thick dark man like straight out of a Bollywood film entered our campus followed by many others, some of whom could be easily identified as scribes. As I went to the gate to receive him, he saw through me and hurried past. He seemed to be asking for the manager. I thought he was looking for me, the Managing Trustee. As someone else from his own entourage was introduced to him as the manager, I stopped in my tracks. On enquiring from the scribes following him, I learnt that he was a minister of Assam heading a legislative committee on unemployment.

As one of our weavers, who heads the weaving organisation, tried to reply to his and his team's queries, I realised there was something amiss. Releasing my loud voice from my height that is a few inches taller than most in the region, I declared that the weaving centre had nothing to do with the government and no government funds had gone into it.

The person who had identified himself as manager—actually he was the manager of the District Industries Commission—reacted sharply. 'Why? Aren't you registered with the government as an SSI? So, how can you say this has nothing to do with the government?' I retorted, 'We also register our vehicles with the government, but that does not make it theirs. Does it?'

The minister asked the manager what was the matter. 'Sir, I have often offered them schemes but they refuse.' I clarified that the only time the DIC had offered us help was to get a 50 per cent subsidy on the bamboo and wood looms that we had bought three years ago. But we had refused as the looms had already been purchased with grants from elsewhere. The minister, seeing that his department may get exposed if such clarifications kept appearing, came to his rescue and asked him to look after our interests and offer us some schemes.

Another of the men in his entourage tried to get even with me for the embarrassment I had caused to his minister. He asked me, 'What is the meaning of the notice not allowing any weapons inside the campus? How can you do that?'

'This is private property and we can very well decide on the rules here', I said. Lest another of my statements start off an embarrassment, another MLA dressed in Islamic attire, pulled this man away telling him, 'Did you not hear what this man (meaning me) said? He said he did not want subsidy on the looms that he had already purchased from grants, understood? Do you understand what kind of a person he is? Come, let us go. This is no place for people like you and I out here.'

The brazenness of the attempt to fraud behind the incident makes me wonder what impression the minister must have got about the government funding of the weaving centre, if I had not intervened and allowed the Assistant Managing Trustee to complete the task of explaining. As a rural illiterate woman, would she have mustered the courage to spill the beans on the DIC manager? I think not. I am still not sure if our registration will get renewed, as it is an important document for us to get bank loans without collateral.

Cocking a Snook

The repeated defiance of law and the absence of action against officials have led to a brazenness that I have not seen elsewhere. Despite the Supreme Court's orders, none of the old and destitute people got their old age pension or the Annapurna ration for more than three years. It is not that the authorities did not know about it. I frequently reminded them, hoping that the letterhead of 'Advisor to the SC Commissioners' may hasten some corrective action. Every three months I kept sending complaint to one official higher, right up to Dispur. I received no reply. Nor did the beneficiaries get their dues until recently after three years, by when many of the old people had died.

In fact, in the discharge of my duties during my five years of service as Advisor to the SC Commissioners, I wrote several letters to higher authorities thinking that reports of malpractices may not reach up to them, and by performing my duty things would get better for the poor. But as I said, *never* have I received a reply. In fact the brazen defiance of orders from Delhi, many of my friends tell me, is an anti-colonial reaction sunk into the bureaucracy. The defiance would only get worse by reminding them of Supreme Court orders!

On 8 March 2011, when many months of cajoling the government did not work, the SC Commissioners on Right to Food convened a JCE to look into the violations of SC orders on the Right to Food in the camps of the internally displaced. Three of us from the civil society kept waiting with dates every month for the three government officials who were to have been members of the JCE. After many reminders they had sent the name of one officer. But when I asked him and later his boss for the other names, I was summarily told that I must not approach them directly. All communications must strictly come from the SC to the Chief Secretary. Sixteen months later, the JCE has still not been held as the government of Assam is yet to nominate the three officials!

Communalisation of Bureaucracy

Behaviour as mentioned above is not just because of the brazenly defiant attitude towards the SC. I suspect part of it was also because it would provide relief to members of the non-indigenous communities which is seen to be against the interests of the state. The officers, despite being sworn to uphold the Constitution of India, show their inhuman attitudes towards women and children by defying the Constitutional provisions.

My suspicion arises from many incidents and gets confirmed every few days. On one occasion, I was with the SC Commissioners who was begging the Chief Secretary for some improvement in the conditions of the refugee camps especially for children and women. The then Chief Secretary bent low to speak into the SC Commissioners' ears in a conspiratorial tone, 'This community (identity withheld) is still okay and we feel may agree to 10,000 rupees as rehabilitation grant. But look at the cheek of the other (identity again withheld), they are asking for 50,000! They think that money grows on trees.' At ₹50,000 a family, these 1,000 families could have been easily rehabilitated at ₹ 5 crore, a sum the Chief Secretary had used to fund the renovation of the Circuit House where we had been housed for the night!

In another incident, a DC was accompanying the Chairperson of the National Commission for Protection of Child Rights (NCPCR). She had just met more than 10 children in the internally displaced persons (IDPs) camp of a community displaced in a communal frenzy nearly 15 years ago. None of them had ever been to the only school there in a shack called an EGS school with one teacher for 250 children.

'Please, Sir, can you arrange for some schools, so that these children can study?' the chairperson asked the DC.

'I know this community very well, Ma'm. Even if we get them schools, they will never go to school', replied the man heading the district administration.

Half an hour later, the functionary of an NGO accompanying the NCPCR Chairperson showed her the destitution of some households and informed her that some women were going into prostitution to feed their fatherless children.

Piped up our man again, 'Ma'm these (community name withheld) women are like that only. They will do anything for sex. Which other mother will leave their child and go out for prostitution?'

The Chairperson was disgusted with his attitude and asked the NGO functionary as to how the NGO work with such people at the helm of affairs in the district. When I heard of this incident I decided to hold a press conference to expose the DC, but better sense prevailed as we did not wish to start another communal clash in a place sitting on a tinderbox all the time!

Bureaucracy Goes Scotfree

An incident was narrated by my friend who retired as a chief engineer of Public Health Engineering (PHE) from an autonomous council that had been in the news for corruption involving humungous amounts of money. He had noticed his staff getting restive and walked out to find out what was the matter. They asked him whether they would get their salaries or not. He found that they had not been paid for the past three months! He enquired of his Superintending Engineer who was responsible for the salaries. He found that the executive member (EM) of the autonomous council had cut ₹ 2 crore from their salaries. He decided to intervene and asked the EM when their legitimate salaries would be released. 'What is the problem?' the EM asked him. 'When poor people have been suffering for so long, what is the problem with your staff sharing some of their money?"

Suspecting that the council must have used up the money to make up for the delay in some other project, he once again asked him, 'Since they are upset, when can I tell them they will get their back dues?'

'What do you mean by back dues? Every department has contributed for the welfare of the people here. Is your department special? Tell them that this is their contribution. And let me remind you, we have not cut your salary!"

In another case, one of his clerks had been caught for not having deposited the PF contribution in the PF account for many years. My friend took him to the EM who he found was related to him. 'You should not have done this. You will deposit the money rightfully, won't you?" he was asked. The accused nodded his head in acceptance and the case was over. No FIR, and no action. As long as my friend worked there, the money never got deposited. His official complaints, like mine, may not have been worth the effort of replying! 'Why don't you go to the police?' maybe an innocent question that I ask of the numerous people who demand our intervention in getting justice. The answer is invariably the same, 'Sir, we are poor. Where will we get so much of money?' No wonder the police department always heads the list of the most corrupt department, just ahead of the health department, according to the Transparency International Surveys (TIS).

I must concede, though, that the police department is the *only* department that has invariably acted on my complaints or have helped me. I am, however, not telling that they solved the case or managed to help the person, but invariably act they did. Their investigations are so sloppy that even a dry rock would feel like an eel in their hands! And worse, on an occasion, when we asked help for a woman to get possession of her child, they feared an antagonist crowd and even asked us to send some of our boys with them in their jeep at night!

Not many months ago, one of my young colleagues frantically rang up informing us that there was a rumour that the militants may burn our field office. Coming on the heels of the NREGS public hearing, when one of our bikes had been burnt, we had no way to reach out to the young team in the field as there was a bandh in the district. We tried to call friends in the area, but what if it is too late? I decided to call up the SP of the district. 'You do not know how to work. It was okay until now. But why did you have to do this public hearing? You have made too many enemies. They say that you must not lift a stone that you cannot carry. Now what? Since you have called me, I know that I will have to send my meagre force in the area, but where is your support now? As a brother I am cautioning you, you never asked me how to work or else I would have taught you. This is a wild jungle that does not understand your kind of people.'

Within minutes, many of our friends from the local students unions had called to tell us that they were there at our field office and we need not worry. I wished I had not asked for help from the SP as I could have avoided hearing the sermon from someone who goes around in a Scorpio that, if rumours are to be believed, is 'gifted' by the ruling party to him as one of the many given to all SPs.

Doctors' Apathy

Being a medical doctor myself and my organisation working in the health sector, it is possible that I see more corruption in this department than others. For a profession that people still think of as godly, I wonder how it has slipped into the morass it is in. That doctors ask patients to buy medicines from the pharmacy outside when the medicines are available in their stock is common knowledge. It has also been proven in one of our recent studies. Doctors often do not send their indents in time or do it inadequately, thanks to the influence of pharmacies. It is such a well-known problem that the minister decided to send a drug-kit of a fixed quantity to every state dispensary to overcome the problem.

Last year, I was told of a woman who was complaining of something coming out of her birth passage and that she wished to see me. As I was travelling I asked one of my colleagues to show her to the gynaecologist at the nearby town. A week later, the woman came to see me again. I saw her prescription by the gynaecologist suggesting surgery for her Prolapse Uterus. They said it will cost ₹18,000 which she was unable to raise. I said I understand what they have to face, but I could see no other way as we could never prove why she had not been operated.

'But can't you examine me once, maybe I do not need a surgery?' she said.

'See, I do not have a clinic where I can examine you privately. Since the gynaecologist has already examined you and made a diagnosis, I do not think you need another internal examination,' I reasoned.

'No, she never examined me', the patient insisted.

'She never took you in and checked you from inside?' I asked.

'No, I insisted. But she said, "If you are not ready to spend ₹18,000, why should I waste my time? You arrange for the money and I will check after that"!'

I was more appalled as I thought that the gynaecologist was one of the better doctors in town as some years ago, she had treated my wife rather well! That poor people have to face the brunt of the doctors is the double jeopardy that they face. They not only attract an unfair share of illnesses thanks to the poor diets that they can afford, but also have to end up paying more for their misfortunes than many like us who can afford more.

In another case, a doctor in a state dispensary charged ₹3,000 for a normal delivery. When the child refused to come out, waited for a full day before he transferred the woman to another state hospital. There too, they could not do anything and only the next day did they send her to a private hospital. By then, the baby had died and the mother had gone into sepsis. She survived after a long battle. Although the Medical Superintendent in this case did take some action, we have not been able to make even a small dent.

In a similar case, another child whose head had got stuck while coming out of his mother's womb, died in the process but the ignominy of carrying such a child stuck at such a position was of no concern to the medical staff. As she was transferred from one state dispensary to another, no one wanted to touch her without the family agreeing to pay at least ₹3,000. After travelling to three state health centres with doctors at each place and having spent ₹2,000 on transportation, the family gave in and paid ₹2,500 more to the good doctor who delivered her finally of her misery!

The case of a husband who had travelled all the way to Guwahati to depose before NHRC was another classic. He had admitted his wife suffering from malaria to the civil hospital at Bongaigaon. This is actually a 30-bedded community health centre supposed to be authorised for rural areas but situated at the edge of the town to save a teetering sate economy in the pre-NRHM days from going bankrupt. She was told that she was very sick and serious and urgently needed a bottle of blood. As her husband's or daughter's blood did not match hers, the doctor told them to meet his man at his private chambers and that he would be able to help out for ₹2,500. The husband did what he was asked. But the blood 'donor' said that he could come only the next day. So, instead, the husband said in his deposition, they decided that instead of taking the risk with some unknown's blood, they would try to get some relatives to donate blood.

So he collected blood from one of his relatives using the facilities of a private hospital en route and carried the blood to the civil hospital. 'If she was so serious, why did the doctor never come to see her again?' he asked. The whole day no one but the nurses attended the patient. The next day, he went to ask the doctor to see his wife. 'Go and get a doctor from the same hospital where you got the blood from to see her!' reprimanded the doctor. The link was clear to this man and he wanted action against the doctor. When asked for a reaction by the Commission members, the Director of Health Services denied the presence of any such hospital in the town and hence said that the complaint should be dismissed. Obviously officially there is no civil hospital as all of them are rural 30-bedded hospitals!

Despite the fact that NRHM has transformed access to state medical services in the past five years or so, it has not been able to do anything against corruption among medical personnel. No one who wishes to terminate her pregnancy is told that it is her legal right to get it. Instead she has to shell out a few thousand rupees to get it done by someone within the state system. There are allegations of private hospitals keeping the state service doctors happy. Why else, it is asked, must centres supposed to provide 24×7 services still not provide services on one pretext or the other?

A late night meeting with medical representatives in my neighbouring town was very revealing. They told me that except three doctors who accepted nothing except medicine samples, that too is banned by statute, every doctor in the town, whether in the public or the private sector, was paid by the medical representatives to prescribe their companies' medicines. The companies had laid out elaborate system to track sales with incentives. I knew about travel jaunts for self and family offered to doctors, of sponsoring medical conferences, and of companies paying EMIs for ACs and cars for doctors. What was new information to me was that doctors were now openly demanding that the companies pay for things like jewellery, tuition fees of their children, and for renovation of houses, chambers, or hospitals too! In fact we found that one doctor had focussed on one particular brand of an antibiotic injection of Ceftriaxone sold at almost double the rates of other companies. This doctor would save the empty vials of the antibiotic administered during the day. He would ask the company representative to come to his hospital and demand ₹100 for each vial that he had emptied! Companies would also give the doctors prescription pads capable of making carbonless copies and each prescription of their brand was handed back to the representatives to prove to their paymasters that the monthly 'retainership' had not gone waste.

Civil Society, you too?

Nowadays it is good to hear about civil society getting together to fight corruption. There must still be some 'mad' people who are yet to give in to corruption. But I do not think there are too many to make a difference. Of those in the movements, maybe, but again, not as a rule, but as an exception! Amongst the NGOs, there may be a few, but that also is a matter of time because the systems are getting to be such that there seems to be little option but to join the bandwagon.

In Assam, to register a society, invariably one needs to pay up at least a few thousand rupees to the Registrar's office or else keep waiting endlessly. To remain registered every three years as per the law, one needs to pay up according to the funds you have received. A friend in the khadi sector, an extremely honest Gandhian, in all his honesty confided that his Board preferred to pay ₹8,000 to the Registrar's office than to listen to his dictats and risk discontinuation of their funding! I have met only one NGO leader to date who said he never had to pay for the registration of his society!

Last year, around 40 NGOs registered for exemption under Section 12A of the Income Tax Act in my neighbouring district. Knowledgeable sources said that each one paid ₹20,000 to get the job done quickly. As they were expecting grants from a 'national level funding agency', they were ready to pay any amount. Otherwise

NGOs take ages to receive exemptions under Section 12A from the Income Tax authorities. I know of some who have been waiting for as long as seven years!

But, to come back to these 40 NGOs, what was this 'national level funding agency' that was ready to fund them? An agency with a website had been travelling the length and breadth of Assam and Arunachal Pradesh carrying out awareness campaigns and urging NGOs to become a member of a national level NGO forum by paying up an amount by next day. If you did not have an NGO, you could conceive it on the spot and name it. You need to, however, ensure that it is registered under the same name later. The 'national level NGO forum', as a funding agency, would then give a grant of 20 to 100 times the membership amount by a post-dated cheque given to them on the spot to 'allow you to write a proposal worth the amount and to open an NGO if not existing already'. It was so lucrative that many people were lured. The people from the 'national level NGO' had hired some locals also and even kept an office open for a month or so, and then they vanished. NGOs brought this incident to light, but they were not ready to register a complaint or hand over the cheques or their photocopies as proof. They only wanted an assurance that they had not been duped altogether. The photos of the people on their web site matched with those taken by NGOs with their mobile cameras. But the NGO got away by denying the allegations. The intelligence agencies also could not do anything as none of the NGOs was ready to testify. As some of them did get some money from the deal probably kept the hope open. The 'national level NGO' which had its headquarters in Delhi and a branch office in Chennai, made crores in its trip, enough to allow some cheques to pass so that they can carry out another heist at a later date.

Conclusion

When every section of the society, including the civil society, has lost its sense of ethics, where does one start from? Where does one place the blame? Should one blame the government alone? Or do we blame the poor who may perish if they do not succumb? The fact that the 'payer is equally guilty as the payee' in the eyes of the law also prevents anyone from bringing bribery to light.

My recent experience does not allow me to appreciate the extent of corruption elsewhere in the country. Hence it will be unfair to think that Assam is worse off than other states. But surely we could have done far better with a better sense of social probity and ethics. We have a neighbour in Mizoram where day-to-day corruption simply does not exist and you can see the government rule book followed in almost all the schemes. One can actually ask anyone on the road and ask if s/he has ever been asked for a bribe and may never get a 'yes'. The Anganwadis under the Integrated Child Development Services (ICDS) actually deliver 300 to 325 days of supplementary nutrition as compared to the SC ruling of 300 days and Assam actually delivering no more than three months in any year.

In Tripura even if the society level institutions have not been as exemplary as in Mizoram, we see much of the money of central government schemes actually reach the rural poor. I have met rural tribal youth rattling off the correct rates of every item that is distributed under the Public Distribution System (PDS) simply because that is the rate at which they receive their entitlements month after month. Contrast it with Assam where kerosene oil is sold even in the urban areas at two rupees above the government rates! The good situation in Tripura may be due to some exemplary chief ministers of Communist-led governments, who were seen to be scrupulously honest in their behaviour unlike the corruption that engulfed West Bengal and led to the downfall of the Communists there.

Anna Hazare's movement may have caught the imagination of everyone in the country, but in Mizoram it is a non-starter. A society that has its ideal in the Mizo code of ethics revolving around 'Tlawmngaihna', an untranslatable term meaning to be hospitable, kind, unselfish, and helpful to others on the part of everyone, cannot understand the fuss to be honest. Tlawmngaihna, to my Mizo friends, stands for the compelling moral force which finds expression in self-sacrifice for the service of others. It is no wonder, therefore, that one can still find unmanned shops and stalls in Mizoram. The customer checks the price and deposits the money into the box kept for the purpose. Auditors may not agree with my assessment of Mizoram as the least corrupt state in India. According to them, the accounting standards may not be up to the mark. This is simply because the high level of ethics and probity has prevented the need for well-documented expenditure! A Mizo friend was ready to wager a bet that at least 95 per cent of his ICDS centres would be giving the correct entitlements to children. He was not proud of his administrative skills or his well monitored and audited system. Instead, he laid the credit at the door of the society which 'will never stoop to steal the entitlements of the poor or mothers and children!' That is what an honesty of culture can bring about. I wish I could say that all tribal cultures are equally honest. Meghalaya, Nagaland, Arunachal Pradesh, and parts of Manipur have predominantly tribal populations, but their politicians and bureaucrats can give the Yediyurappas, Rajas, and Kalmadis a run for their money!

Tripura, as I mentioned earlier, has a Left government for some time that appears to a majority of its people as genuinely concerned about the poor. It may not be equally sensitive to the needs of its indigenous people who have become a minority since Independence, but its worst detractors who feel that the government machinery favours the Left's supporters will agree that a lot of the money does trickle down to the village level.

Sikkim may not be anywhere near Mizoram as far as honesty is concerned, and not half as oriented to the poor as Tripura. But it has managed to demonstrate that if the government has the will, a way will be found to surmount the problems that keep development away from the poor and marginalised. I do not buy the argument that it can develop well as it is a small state, because one can compare it with smaller entities like North Cachar Hills and Karbi Anglong

Autonomous Districts to know how autonomy not utilised properly can be ruinous even at smaller levels. The best bet is to combine the experiences that have improved things in Tripura, Mizoram, and Sikkim. Concern for the poor is necessary amongst the political leadership, as in Tripura. A positive political and administrative will is necessary for development of all as in Sikkim. But what can sustain such things is an acculturation of sorts, of creating a culture of scrupulous honesty and social commitment in the people of our country, as in Miozram. That will take development further.

It is time for us to get 'mad'. Be 'mad' at corruption, meaning that we need to 'make a difference', and *now*! That we do not ask or accept bribes is not enough any longer. We need to stop others indulging in such malpractices. *Now!* It is not enough to avoid making payments by going through brokers or agents, but we need to spend time and challenge the system ourselves. We cannot expect the rich to correct the system, as they probably got rich in the first place by giving in. We must not hope that the poorest will stop paying bribes to the development officials or else they will not get even the 10 per cent that helps them to sustain their family. But if we in the middle rungs decide and take up the cudgels to restore the glory of our 5,000-year old civilisation, the system will surely feel the pinch. More importantly, most of the government officials happen to be amongst us, our relatives and friends, and I am sure things shall fall in the right tracks sooner than later.

A Plea for Consensual Governance

Vijayalakshmi Brara

The Iroquois League was a model social order in many ways superior to the white man's culture of the day. Its democratic form of government more nearly approached perfection than any that has been tried to date. -- Elmore Reaman, 1967

On the issue of governance, historians and political scientists alike have focussed on military engagements and defining and re-defining territorial boundaries. They have not given much emphasis on cultural interaction and expansion as well as the cultural ways in which societies function. There is need to pick up the threads from the cultures across the globe to understand the governance systems of each region, rather than through wars and conquests.

By re-calling Iroquois confederacy, I want to bring in what we seem to be losing—the governance of consensus. Development, conflict and governance have become the key words in the discourse vis-a-vis north-east India. But we keep forgetting that this region has a very strong tradition of bringing about consensus and resolving issues even before the conflict arises.

Iroquois confederacy has had the longest oral constitution dating back to 13th to 14th century. It was only written down in 1917. The thrust of the Constitution is on public opinion and public consensus and the clearly defined role of leaders. A major criterion is that the leader cannot earn more than the modest earnings. Thomas Jefferson said that Iroquois is the best government since it is the least government.

We have had the cultures of consensus in Manipur. But either deliberately or due to ignorance we have seeped in the kind of governance which is mainly interested to rule rather than govern.

In this paper I will bring in those forgotten elements of consensus and appeal to the policy makers to integrate them into the so called modern democratic system of ours to enable us to wipe out the elements of conflict. We need to usher in a North-East Confederacy in the lines of Iroquois Confederacy.

Picking Up Cultural Threads

On the issues of governance, the historians and political scientists alike have focussed on military engagements and defining and re-defining territorial boundaries. They have not given much emphasis on cultural interaction and expansion as well as the cultural ways in which the society functions. There is need to pick up the threads from cultures across the globe to understand their governance systems, rather than wars and conquests.

The cultural component should form the basic premise if we are to understand the governance ethos of any society. Myths, legends, folklores, belief systems, notions of collectives, systems of hierarchies, value systems, systems of social order, and consensus as well as the society's own law of progression need to be studied to understand the functioning of the State structure.

The term 'State', according to Geertz, has at least three etymological themes condensed within it: (i) status, in the sense of rank standing; (ii) pomp in the sense of splendour and display; and (iii) governance, in the sense of regency and regime. The third element, to the exclusion of the other two, has come to dominate modern political discourse. Such an approach does not fully explicate all the elements that constitute the concept of 'State'. He propounded the concept of 'Theatre State', which involves studying the state structure of a given society through the elements of culture, an understanding of rituals, and observance of symbolic codes in interpersonal behaviour among people and in considering people's perception of their state, king, and society. So, it evolves from and revolves around a comprehensive understanding of a given society.

According to Hocart's perception, traditional structures or polity is not a system of governance, but an organisation to promote life, fertility, and prosperity. Only gradually has its scope enlarged and its functions modified, until it has become a centralised means of organising the activities of society. Denouncing theories based purely on economic factors, Hocart says that these are a very small fragment of life, and the pursuit of wealth is not one that inspires much zeal for common good. One cannot build a State on the narrow basis of prices and wages, but only on the widest cooperation for life. The reason for our failed nations and ever-increasing demand for homeland in our region is because we have not been able to understand the emergence of State and the issues of governance from the cultural point of view. Instead, our understanding of the State structure has been based on authority and a jural institution. This notion has debarred us from encompassing the traditions of the widest cooperation of life. I am of the view that if the cultural notions of State of the North-East could have been studied and incorporated into our policy frameworks encompassing the North-East into the pan-Indian fold, issues of conflict and separation would have been relegated to the realm of non-issues. This exercise can be initiated even now and we can start by learning how our people in the North-East resolve their issues and incorporate them in our endeavour to resolve conflicts of this region.

What is Our Problem?

The problem is not India's experience in the North-East but the North-East's experience in India. Let me dwell a bit on the past. B.R.

Ambedkar, with his other colleagues, while framing the Constitution of India, formulated the policy on North-East with the good intention of preserving the indigenous polity and traditional institutions. According to Honourable Rev. J.J.M. Nichols Roy

> The hill districts inhabited by tribal hill people will under this Constitution be able to develop themselves according to their genius and culture. The result I believe will be charming if these autonomous districts are nurtured to develop themselves in their own way without disturbing the main purpose of unity underlying the constitution presented in this draft.

In our present context the key words are 'nurtured' and 'unity'. I am sometimes made to feel that the aspect of nurturing was relegated to the background for a very long time, with the result that the institutions, the polity, as well as the people were left on their own. Left on their own, how could they integrate with the pan-Indian psyche? This resulted in the models of autonomous district councils and the Sixth Schedule not having the desired result. Alienation has seeped deep in the hearts of the people of this region giving rise to self-assertions and the desire to be separated from the rest of India.

Geographically, North-East is connected to the rest of India through what we call a 'chicken neck'. It aptly symbolises the precarious relation of this region with the rest of India since the time the British left and the Indian government took over. Why could not the Indian government integrate this region into pan–Indian fold? I picked up the following reaction from www.theeconomist.com which expresses a similar sentiment.

> Fifty-eight years into India becoming republic on 26th Jan 1950, the entire North-East India does not picture in what the term 'Indian'—in culture, in principle, in anything in front of the whole world. The vision 'India' as proclaimed by Central

> Govt does not include the North-East India at all, instead the govt created a separate 'North-East India Vision 2020'. It's the central Indian govt which is still alienating the North-East India from India becoming a single country. Are North-East Indians not Indians? Or the word 'Indians' to the North-East Indians a blessing/tagging to identify like household pet? Why Indian govt is able to create rest of Indian states/territories to forgo the concept of kingdoms in the past? Why not to the North-East Indian states?

So, what has happened over a period of time? For a long time we were embroiled in dual classification of being Indian and at the same time not 'really being one'; we did not know! The Constitution makers gave us the autonomy to nurture our own culture and Institutions. While we were happy with our world we were told that the Indian government is bringing their model of what is called democracy to this land. We started understanding the whole gamut of terminologies in the package of Panchayati Raj. Instead of chiefs and clan representatives we started having MLAs and ministers. In other words, the polity involving people was replaced by institutions.

The Policy Lacuna

Now, why did Ambedkar or Jawaharlal Nehru not decide to leave us alone in the first place? Henceforth every debate on resistance by the people was done away with force. One is not denying the fact that violence and conflict were very much part of the tradition. But so were the very effective culture of consensus. But somehow the dominant discourse of conflict remained on the surface with modern paradigms of identity, territory, rule, and power, and culture of consensus were put out of the debate by the modern political gurus jockeying for their place in governance.

Various tribes of this land have been living together since time immemorial. There have been wars and conquests among them.

The reason for their existence till today, however, has its basis in the way the consensus has been brought about by seeking public opinion and people's participation, what we call today in our modern document of Vision 2020 as 'inclusive governance'. On moving across various tribes in north-east India, one can document extensive areas of traditions of resolutions. These traditions need be brought into the forefront and incorporated into the modern institutions of governance if we are interested in addressing the issues of development, conflict, and governance.

The Indian State should have endeavoured to help create a North-East Confederacy with the traditions of governance as laid down by various tribes of this region and then incorporated it into the Indian Constitution. Then the progression of societies in the North-East would have been along with the Indian psyche. In other words, there would have been neither any need for 'mainstreaming' the North-East, nor create a separate *North East Vision 2020.*

The political processes in Africa can bring in some parallels to north-east India. Both being predominantly tribal societies are dwelling with the 'progressive democracies of exclusion' and 'traditional structures of inclusion'. According to Oya O.E. there is general agreement in most African countries that coups must end, corruption must be rooted out, and economies must be restored. There is less agreement among Africans about the meaning of 'democracy'. Many Africans believe that the larger issue of governance is related to the general conditions in African countries. Some African scholars declare that there were traditional forms of democracy, autocracy, monarchy, and oligarchy in state-organised societies as well as stateless societies in their pre-colonial history. They assert that African traditional political systems functioned not because of their forms, but because they fulfilled the felt needs of societies. According to this argument, the important factor was 'political authority' derived from a 'jural community' and defined as the widest grouping within which there is a moral obligation and a means ultimately to settle disputes.

African scholars insist increasingly that western ideas about democracy are specifically rooted in the notion of political and social rights for individuals whereas the reality of Africa is still one in which 'collectivities' or 'ethnic' groups, rather than individuals, demand social justice. In this context what matters is respect for African cultures and languages and ethnic concerns in the distribution of their countries' or world resources. These views are now being linked to the conviction that African traditional leaders and important personages should join politicians in governing their societies. Moreover, these demands come from urbanites as well as rural folk.

The Iroquois Confederacy

It is in this light that I would like to recall Iroquois Confederacy. *The Constitution of the Five Nations or the Iroquois Book of the Great Law* was written by Arthur C. Parker, archaeologist of the State Museum in New York in 1915. The Confederacy survives after some 500 or 600 years. It was originated by people that the white Americans mistakenly considered as 'savages'. Some sources place the origin of the Five Nation Confederacy as early as A.D. 1390, but others insist that it was established around AD 1450–1500. In any case, it was well before any possible contamination by European invaders. Early explorers and colonists found the Iroquois well established, as they had been for many generations – with a democratic government, with a form of religion that acknowledged a Creator in heaven, and with a strong sense of family which was based on, and controlled by, their women. Incidentally, the Iroquois are a matrilineal society.

From inception, there were Five Nations discussed in this Constitution. In about 1715, Tuscarora Nation, once part of the Iroquois peoples earlier, moved up from North Carolina to avoid warfare with the invading white settlers, and were adopted into the Confederacy. At this point in time, the Iroquois controlled many parts of the current eastern states from their homelands in what is now New York State. The original Five Nations were:

- Mohawk: People possessors of the flint
- Onondaga: People on the hills
- Seneca: Great hill people
- Oneida: Granite people
- Cayuga: People at the mucky land

Tuscarora: Shirt wearing people, became the Sixth Nation.

Dekanawida, born near the Bay of Quinte, in south-eastern Ontario, Canada, is generally acknowledged as the founder of the Confederacy of the Five Nations. During his travels, he associated himself with a Mohawk tribal lord in what is now New York, and named him Hahyonhwatha (Hiawatha) (he who has misplaced something, but knows where to find it). Hiawatha left his family and friends and joined Dekanawida in his travels becoming his chief spokesman.

One legend has it that Dekanawida, while being brilliant, had a speech impediment, and depended on Hiawatha to do his public speaking for him. Together they travelled the length and breadth of the lands on the south shores of lakes Erie and Ontario, as well as the river to the sea, now known as St. Lawrence. These were the homelands of tribes with a common heritage, but who had been warring with one another for many years. Dekanawida united them into a league of nations that we now call the Iroquois League.

Let me dwell only on some parts dealing with the ethics of leadership and the important role of women in making or breaking their chiefs. The women heirs of the Confederated Lordship titles were called Royaneh (Noble). It is written in their constitution that the Royaneh women, holders of a Lordship title, select one of their sons as a candidate. They select as chief one who is trustworthy, of good character, of honest disposition, manages his own affairs, supports his own family, if any, and has proven a faithful man to his Nation.

They aimed for Great Peace and after making the Constitution resolved to bury their differences forever.

> I, Dekanawida, and the Union Lords, now uproot the tallest pine tree and into the cavity thereby made we cast all weapons of war. Into the depths of the earth, down into the deep underearth currents of water flowing to unknown regions we cast all the weapons of strife. We bury them from sight and we plant again the tree. Thus shall the Great Peace be established and hostilities shall no longer be known between the Five Nations but peace to the United People.

Some Important Facets of Iroquois Confederacy

The way the Constitution of Iroquois League was adopted by the Americans it was termed the 'Americanisation of the white people'. Felix Cohen in 1952 defined Americanism as largely a product of the influence of Indian culture on the white European settlers. In an equally bold statement, Jennings (1975) states, 'What white (American) society owes to Indian society, as much as to any other source, is the mere fact of its existence.'

The Iroquois Constitution is the longest existing international constitution in the world. Known as 'The Great Law of Peace', this orally transmitted constitution describes a federal union of six tribes and was put in the written form only in 1715.

Canassatego, speaker for the great council at Onondaga, while advising the white people, recommended that the colonies form a union in common defence under a federal government. 'We are a powerful Confederacy, and by your observing the same methods our wise forefathers have taken, you will acquire much strength and power; therefore, whatever befalls you, do not fall out with one another.'

The confederacy managed their internal affairs without interference from the Grand Council.

Even Marx and Engels drew on Iroquois models to support their theories and designs. Engels, like the American revolutionaries a century earlier, was impressed with the Iroquois' ability to achieve economic equality without coercion and to maintain social consensus without a large state apparatus. It is interesting to note that the roots of American democratic government and Communism came from similar ideologies, one emphasising on individualism and the other on communal holdings. Both key elements were held in balance by the Iroquois. Other scholars see a prototype of the 20th century United Nations in Iroquois' thought and constitution.

Each of the Iroquois nations was represented in the Confederate Council by a lord of the confederacy and one war chief. Their league included a system of checks and balances, and no action could be taken without the approval of all five nations. Their notions of equality and liberty extended to women as well as men. In war, they never enslaved captives but offered to adopt those willing to accept the Great Law. Their own members could be alienated or expelled by not following the Great Law, and a non-member could be adopted by proposal or invitation with approval from the lords.

The image of their leaders and their belief in the system of governance are the major features of their success. In their constitution, the lords of the confederacy are described as mentors and spiritual guides of the people. Their hearts are full of peace and goodwill, and their minds full of yearning for the welfare of the people, including those of future generations. Their words and actions are to be marked by calm deliberation. They must be honest and must have no self-interest. If they become wayward they receive warnings first from the clan women and then from the men. If they persist in negative behaviours, they ultimately lose their position and possibly their life. The lords are poorer than the common people. They own few material possessions, and give away presents or plunder acquired by treaty or war. They are above pettiness and corruption, and show no signs of selfishness.

Public opinion and popular consent were key in maintaining freedom and good government. The power of public opinion was an important reason for Iroquois' lack of oppressive government and class differences, and for the power to impeach officials who offended governing principles.

The Iroquois society was matri-lineal. Women owned the land and the status of their lineage. They owned all possessions of their husbands after marriage except their horses and rifles. They took care of the money. They were the tribe's educators and communicators of tradition. The Lord of the Confederacy was nominated by women who selected him for qualities of trustworthiness, good character, honesty, faithfulness to the people and the nation, support of the family, and good management of personal affairs. There was no state religion, and the religious rites and festivals of each nation were safeguarded against being disturbed or interrupted. Civil duties were separated from those of the religious leaders, and festivals were held in each clan's longhouses.

Some of Our Own Elements of Consensus

Hemkham or cease fire is a custom among the Kukis in the North-East. When one intentionally or unintentionally kills someone, the culprit's family kills a pig in the Chief's house as Hemkham. Hemkham is to be performed as soon as possible to avoid further use of weapons in retaliation. Once Hemkham is performed, both parties are automatically bound by the Law of Hemkham and killing is stopped and arbitrated in a peaceful manner. The murderer has to pay the following for the performance of Hemkham.

i. Selpikhat (one Mithun) for Kosana
ii. Khipichangni (two pieces of bead) for the eyes
iii. Dahpikhat (one Gong) for his Pillow
iv. Pondumkhat (one traditional shawl) for winding sheet

Interestingly, Hemkham has been taken up by Manipur government recently to resolve and prevent communal tensions.

Two Kuki students of North-Eastern Hill University (NEHU), Shillong, on their way to celebrate Christmas at Bongbal Kholen were unfortunately lynched by Nongbrang Meitei Villagers in Thoubal

District of Manipur on 22 December 2009. The two were mistaken for members of the Kuki militant group operating in the area.

Tribal social organizations like Kuki Students' Organisation (KSO), All Naga Studients' Association, Manipur (ANSAM), All Tribal Students' Union Manipur (ATSUM), Kuki Movement for Human Rights (KUMHUR), and Kuki National Army (KNA) blocked NH 39 for a day and some Meitei leaders from United Committee Manipur (UCM) and All Manipur United Clubs Organisation (AMUCO) with the help of the government of Manipur visited the spot and the victims' families. The government asked the Meitei community to perform Hemkham on 31 December 2009. The Nongbram Meiteis performed Hemkham by killing a pig and admitted to their crime before the Court of Bongbal Kholen chief. The matter was resolved between the two parties.

Even shooting by the police commandos on the Kuki populace have been resolved by performing Hemkham.

There are evidence of Manipur having a federal structure during the Meitei kings' rule in the state. The relationship between the Meitei and that of the chiefs in the hills was that of mutual respect and harmony and not dominance by brute force. The hills were allowed to have their own polity aligned with their tradition. There are also documents of peace treaties between various tribes where they have erected tombs with signatures of the chiefs engraved on it. There are also instances where the chiefs of two tribes have drunk water together from the barrel of the gun to symbolise brotherhood.

According to Lanusashi Longkumer, in the socio-cultural and political life of the Nagas oral narration was, and still is, a powerful weapon to prove or disprove, substantiate and support any dispute/ claims or for resolving any dispute or conflict. It is instrumental in peace negotiation or to conduct truce in times of war or confrontation. Pledges and promises made between two conflicting parties ensuing after peaceful negotiations were highly respected and honoured. Dispute over river water between Phom tribe and

Changtongya village of Ao tribe, which could not be resolved by the British, was resolved through dialogue and oath taking.

I tend to agree with Longkumer when he says that modern diplomacies, accords, and agreements need to learn from the time-tested distinct values of transparency, honesty, and truth. Hence the scenario of conflict can be attributed to the modern state, the centralised structures and a system of governance believing in ruling. No system of governance can be based on suspicion towards the leader ruling the people. It will invariably lead to conflict. To quote Thomas Jefferson, 'Experience hath shown that even under the best forms (of government) those entrusted with power have, in time, and by slow operations, perverted it into tyranny'. It is this notion of power and the idea of ruling which has to be removed from the models of governance and make it built through the confidence of the people and through their participation. We need to build our modern institutions from the time-tested cultures of consensus prevalent in our societies.

As Elliot P. Skinner says in his essay on African political cultures, given the false starts and stops that accompany all changes, and a very anthropological truism that not all mutations succeed, no one can really tell whether the new attempts of contemporary Africans to create political systems out of the chequered cloth of traditional authorities and elected ones will succeed. Owusu (1991: 384) holds that 'African democracy may require the integration of indigenous methods of village cooperation with innovative forms of government, combining the power of universal rights with the uniqueness of each district's or nation's own customs and respected traditions'. Lloyd believed that the emergent African political leaders needed to turn the allegiance of the masses from ethnic groups to the State, and from their traditional rulers to the parliamentary leaders, especially when members of the new ruling class, by training and ways of thought, and in styles of life, were divorced from the masses. He advised politicians to recognise the loyalty of people to their traditional leaders, and to involve the latter in the governance of the country. Above all, politicians should not use traditional leaders only for symbolic purposes, thereby running the risk of 'destroying the prestige of the rulers just as did too close an association with the colonial administration in past decades' (Lloyd 1970: 382–412).

It is in this sense that I advocate Iroquois Confederacy. Since one cannot deny the fact that if we had been allowed to be nurtured the way Ambedkar and Rev. Nichols visualised, perhaps we also would have headed towards a similar kind of confederacy for the tribes of the whole of North-East, a confederacy based on consensus rather than conflict. Perhaps we still can.

References

Jennings, Francis. 1975. *The Invasion of America: Indians, Colonialism and the Cant of Conquest.*

Lloyd, Peter C. 1970. 'Nigeria: Background to Nationalism' in James S. Coleman and Carl G. Rosberg Jr. eds. *Political Parties and National Integration in Tropical Africa.* Berkeley: University of California Press, pp. 382–412.

Owusu, Maxwell. 1991.' Democracy and Africa: A View from the Village', *The Journal of Modern African Studies*, 30(3): 384.

The economist.com: Free Analyst, downloaded on 7 November 2009

DEMOCRATIC RIGHTS

Democracy, Development, and Justice: A Gender Perspective

Sukalpa Bhattacharjee

Recent studies on development has posed important challenges to mainstream development studies and policies such as sustainable development, alternative development, participatory development, and reflexive development, and so on. It would be of strategic importance to assess some of the issues raised by the post-development perspective, which is also symptomatic of some of the confusions introduced by the post-modernist wave that swept the social sciences in the 1990s. By most post-development accounts, the 'subject' of development has been proved to be dead. Post-development theory challenges mainstream development theory for its 'pernicious colonisation' of knowledge in what was once referred to as 'underdeveloped' or 'Third World' areas. The crisis of development theory has been described by Colin Leys as being precipitated by the immense unleashing of market forces in the Third World, the failures of Marxism and First World feminism, and the concomitant inability of states to be the 'prime movers' of development that had been the assumption of 'modern' development theory. At the same time the power of social movements to effect systemic change has fallen short of their intended promise (Leys 1996: 7). It is due to the void left by the crisis in both conventional and Marxist development theory that post-development theory stakes its theoretical claims. The polemics of this challenge are organised around a 'post-modernist' attack on the foundationalist and humanist assumptions of the mainstream development theory that emerged in the social sciences in the post-1945 period. It is assumed that both the 'imperialist pretensions' of the Western development apparatus and the failed promise of Marxist alternatives have led to the disenchantment with development theory, projects, and practices.

As the post-development theorists have reminded us, working in development inevitably positions us within a 'development discourse', where, as Ilan Kapoor (2004: 627–47) states, the North's superiority over the South is taken for granted, and Western-style development is the norm. Our encounters with and representations of our 'subjects' are, therefore, coded or framed in terms of an 'us/them' dichotomy. The issue of justice becomes integral to our understanding of development because of an inheritance that Spivak frequently emphasises as the history of imperialism. The idea of development is rooted in the imperialist project and Spivak reminds us of the materialist dimensions of this history, especially the way in which colonialism incorporated the colonies into the international division of labour and thus initiated a process of global inequality and socio-economic impoverishment, particularly in the Third World. According to Spivak, this process continues even today under the rubric of 'globalisation', with women bearing the brunt of the costs. The epistemic violence of imperialism has meant the transformation of the Third World into a sign whose production has been obfuscated to the point that Western superiority and dominance are naturalised (Spivak 1999: 114).

Global conflict and political violence in the contemporary world interrogate development paradigms on the one hand and the theoretical framework of peace initiatives on the other. Many countries have endured decades of armed conflict, and others live under the permanent menace of political violence. Throughout, the gendered impacts of armed conflict and political violence are key issues which remain unresolved. The gendered causes, costs, and consequences of violent conflicts have been under-represented, and often misrepresented. One observes that the image of women in war and conflict literature posit women as victims rather than as actors, largely because of patriarchal structures. Women in fact occupy several roles and create different fates for themselves, as war is also a site of potential change. Women are seldom integrated within processes of peace negotiations at any stage. An analysis of women's roles and the inclusion of women working in conflict situations reveal that women are not only fighters and/or victims, but also negotiators in post-conflict futures. A critical examination of women's participation in formal and informal peace-building activities shows that in most cases women are excluded from formal peace negotiations. Such high-level negotiations are identified as male domains, which means that they also employ discourses and practices that are closer to men's reality than to women's. As a result, women also lack direct influence in the identification of reconstruction priorities that are usually part of a peace agreement. Nevertheless, women have been playing an influential role through their work in grassroots organisations working for peace and reconciliation. From within these organisations, women constantly challenge the authorities and other members of society with demands for peace, non-discrimination, accountability, recognition of human rights, and so on. While always positioned on the margins, these organisations show their ability to mobilise large numbers of women and to translate individual grievances into legitimate social concerns. Moreover, many of them play a significant role in building a new culture of peace at the local level by organising peace education and community-based reconciliation and social reconstruction activities.

Many countries emerging from armed conflict have adopted new constitutions that grant women equal political, social, and economic rights, and many governments have developed new quota systems to ensure women equal representation in decision-making institutions at all levels. However, the implementation of these laws and good intentions often runs into major obstacles. At the government level the problems include lack of financial resources, gender awareness, or political will among the staff. Other major problems are to be found at the social level, where the new discourse of gender equality may run counter to existing social norms on gender roles. In some cases, local authorities and male members of society may discourage or prohibit women from participating in political activities. Moreover, the fact that the division of labour has not changed in favour of women, but rather added to their burden, also poses practical limitations on the possibilities of active involvement of women.

In a post-war situation, the end of war does not signal the end of violations of women's rights. Often many women face more discrimination in reconstruction programmes, sexual and domestic violence in refugee camps, and violence when they attempt to return to their homes. It is reported that in Afghanistan, women of all ethnicities have been compelled to restrict their participation in public life even after the fall of Taliban to avoid being 'targets of violence by armed factions and those seeking to enforce repressive Taliban-era edicts'. Women, especially those living outside Kabul, continue to face serious threats to their physical safety, denying them the opportunity to exercise their basic human rights, and to participate fully and effectively in rebuilding their country.

In Iraq insecurity and fear of sexual violence and abduction keep women in their homes, out of schools, or away from work. Despite being on such vulnerable margins, women have been able to constitute various subjectivities to transform their vulnerability into creative agencies for encounter and redemption.

Therefore, our understanding of women's roles in post-war societies and of their contributions to post-war reconstruction must go beyond the universalistic narrative of 'women's experience of war' and their vulnerability. The specificity and diversity of women's experiences must be acknowledged. Only on the basis of this can we conduct comparative analyses and develop a deeper general understanding of post-war reconstruction from a gender perspective. Such a perspective would involve a shift in the representation of the image of women from vulnerable victims to that of a highly differentiated group of social actors, who possess valuable resources and capacities and who have their own agendas. Women influence the course of things and their actions constitue post-war societies. The reduction of women to both targets and beneficiaries fails to recognise their contributions and leads to their marginalisation.

Gender-specific data as well as gender-focused analyses are also needed to understand women's situation within a gender framework which pays attention to the way gender roles and relationships are continuously constructed and contested by different actors, and which recognises the gender dimension inherent in all aspects of war and post-war reconstruction.

The gender perspective is also relevant for the achievement of sustainable peace. If peace is a structure of expectations based on specific balance of powers, the failure to recognise gender issues may produce new social tensions and contribute to the differentiating struggles over identity, status, and power that are so distinctive for societies which have recently achieved peace. Recent studies have tried to project a gendered interpretation of war and how masculinist narratives of war omit many important issues involving female agencies.

Political realism paints a violent and anarchical picture of the world's socio-political development without taking into account the influence of the non-state actors, but influenced in turn by those developments. When women are acknowledged by political realists they arc seen only as victims and seldom as agents. By projecting the discourses and agenda of only State or elite actors, which, of course, does not include gendered non-State actors in a situation of conflict, one misses out on the very important issue of intimacy in war. In war and conflict situation, particularly ethnic wars, the perpetrator and victim intimately know one another through real contact or imagination. The politics of 'betrayal and resistance' operate at the community level but it is in those intimate moments of war that the actual causes of conflict are to be traced.

Women not only experience such moments through direct acts of violence on them by the perpetrators but also play active roles in addressing such conflicts. One example is the role played by women in the conflict situation in India's north-eastern region. Many women's organisations of north-east India, like the Naga Mothers' Association (NMA), are on a collaborative project either with the State actors or the ones opposing it. NMA has played a mediatory role between the government of Nagaland and the Naga Students' Federation (NSF) on issues of employment. NMA is also responsible for the formation of the Peace Team in 1994. Although women wage peace in conflict situations, reports and studies on the effects of armed conflict tend to incorporate women in the general category of civilians without citing the differences in gendered experience of violence. On the one hand, as members of the civilian population, women experience distinctive economic problems in armed conflict. In many cases, women are separated from men who traditionally may be their sources of income. Many cultural factors exacerbate the economic problems already faced by women. Women are forced to leave their homes or migrate when war or conflicts break out. In the process they are exposed to foreign conditions which render them more vulnerable to accidents, injuries, and rape. This is also a basic dislocation from physical and reproductive health. Further, as internally displaced persons (IDPs) and refugees, women are mistreated in camps and other countries. Mention may also be made of the Sri Lankan situation where, according to Darini Rajasingham-Senanayake

> During two decades of armed conflict in north-east Sri Lanka, women have carved new spaces of agency and new roles as armed combatants, principal income generators or heads of household in the absence of men folk. Will they be pushed back 'into the kitchen' with a return to peace, also often indexed as a return to the pre-war gender status quo?

A similar phenomenon can also be seen in the context of political conflict in Nepal where women suffer tremendous physical and psychological displacement. On the other hand they try to negotiate between warring parties in an alternative civic space.

Women in conflict situations do not represent the official voices of war such as government or military. Therefore, they are non-state actors who exist off-stage but who help either to further a war or critically challenge it. One knows how women have historically served the war process by providing the day-to-day maintenance of war on the one hand and relinquishing male children to the 'cause' on the other. Studies have been conducted to show how women have served as pawns in conflict and war situations as victims of systematic rape, forced prostitution, etc. At the same time women as non-State actors have also served as voices of resistance as in the cases of Meira Paibis (women torch bearers).

The role of women's groups and organisations in north-east India is significant because they are powerful agents of what Swanee Hunt calls 'inclusive security', which she says 'rests on the principle that fundamental social changes are necessary to prevent renewed hostilities'. Conflict does not get resolved just by signing peace accords. Women in post-conflict situation have always worked at the grass roots levels to effect social change. Women execute this role by collaborative approach with government agencies and dominant diplomatic structures, thereby enlarging the civic space for citizen empowerment. Social change that would 'prevent renewed hostilities' can also be effected through the articulation of alternative narratives of physical and spiritual sufferings of human beings in a conflict situation as against the male-centred universalist narratives of war and conflict. 'Gender justice' is often used with reference to emancipatory projects that advance women's rights through legal change, or promote women's interests in social and economic policy. However, the term is rarely given a precise definition and is often used interchangeably with notions of gender equality, gender equity, women's empowerment, and women's rights.

Any definition of gender justice betrays a political position, a set of convictions about what is 'right' and 'good' in human relationships, and how these desirable outcomes may be achieved. Ideologies and conventions about women's subordination to men and the family are often rooted in assumptions about what is 'natural' or 'divinely ordained' in human relationships. The implication is that the interpretations of the terms are simply not amenable to human improvement. These perspectives on women's rightful subordination are legitimated not by appeals to justice but by socially embedded convictions about honour and propriety—convictions felt to be beyond the realm of justice. It is not surprising, therefore, that concepts of gender justice that seek to enhance women's autonomy or rights in relation to men are controversial and arouse intense debate.

Experts state that gender justice includes unique elements that go beyond related concepts of justice in class or race terms, which complicate both its definition and enactment.

First, women cannot be identified as a coherent group along with other sets of disempowered people such as ethnic minorities or socially excluded immigrants.

Second, unlike any other social group, relationships between women and men in the family and community are a key site of gender-specific injustice, and, therefore, any strategy to advance gender justice must focus on power relations in the domestic or 'private' context.

Third, the patriarchal mindsets and social relations that are produced in the private sphere are not contained there, but infuse most economic, social, and political institutions. In fact, justice itself, in its conception and administration, is very often gendered, responding to a patriarchal standard derived from the domestic arena.

A critique of a World Bank (WB) document from a gendered perspective will explain the delinking of development discourse from justice. One cannot but adumbrate the fact that community-based management of resources is based on a gendered division of labour in the case of north-east India. The document speaks of the creation of a platform for interaction between the relevant stakeholders ultimately leading to desired institutional reforms. It, however, ignores the role that women can play. Given that there are matrilineal societies and maternal control over community resources, the document does not voice concerns of mothers who engage themselves as unequal partners in a discourse of development. The World Bank completely effaces women's discourses of sharing labour, resources, and outputs in the local level management of productive activity. The basic work of river basin management, inter-state cooperation, hydropower, and flood management, as it is programmed in the said document, keeps women completely out of its purview. But this effacement of women is often covered up while the document identifies the ill-effects of developmental process. Such ill-effects are catalogued as deforestation, mining and quarrying, jhuming, charcoal-making, construction of reservoirs and dams, over-harvesting of medicinal plants, drying up of wetlands, and over-fishing and pollution of water bodies, all of which puts the blame on the communities. Seemingly, the silence on women in the document serves the purpose of pointing to those actors who are supposedly responsible for depletion of environmental resources. It is common knowledge that the labour-intensive method of utilisation of environmental resources is employed mostly by women in the North-East. The document, however, tacitly holds them responsible for such depletion. This strategy of silence and tacit statements about the state of environment in the region obliterates the role of agencies in the whole process of development. Planners point out that the absence of any agency exercise on the part of people themselves marks how the development strategy condones itself from enabling people. This absence of reciprocity between strategic thinkers and the people, for whom it is thought out, gets compounded with a reductionist notion of people understood from an already determined set of priorities. Women being more than half the sky, their wellbeing and participation cannot be posited in terms of human vs natural dichotomy. If such a dichotomy is maintained, it creates other kinds of dichotomies such as stakeholders and funders. The document articulates such dichotomies in so many ways when it attempts to identify the deficits of development in the North-East. It focuses on two such deficits: a credibility deficit, a failure of policy promises to be matched by outcomes; and an adequacy deficit the failure to adequately compensate the losers from resource exploitation and ensure that benefits are adequately distributed. In both these cases, recognition of the role of women in thwarting such consequences of development policy could have given a different picture of reality. The different picture lies in the fact that the public patriarchy of institutional economy, as outlined in the document, depends heavily on women's participation in the productive activity of the North-East. The process of building up cultural capital and feeding it into a circulating global economy is a process of commodification of natural resources that the document suggests. But how can these extraordinary and specific cultural resources be sustained within a trajectory of cash–contract–tourist economy without commodification is the moot question that concerns the gender perspective. The document continuously curbs and transmutes the existing forms of social and cultural practices of the region to fit them to the economistic drill, which is a return to a Hobbesian notion of order. How is such an order given content in the document is an ideological ploy, whereby, the relationship between the North-East and South-East and East Asia is given a phantasmal description in terms of fly-by-night trading and connectivity. The idea of geographical contiguity with the Asian Development Bank (ADB)-built trans-Asian road, rail, and air connectivity now replaces the old nationalist myth of integration and substitutes it with a signifier of regional economic integration through bodies like Bay of Bengal Initiative for Multi-Sectoral Technical and Economic Cooperation (BIMSTEC). The document further makes the claim that the concentrated rents (benefits) accruing from natural resources influence the kind of institutions that evolve. It claims that the prospect of large and rapid gains from natural wealth tends to reorient administrative priorities from concerns about the size of the pie (growth) to concerns about the share of the pie (distribution). Unfortunately, such concern about sharing the pie nowhere includes women as the real agents for income generation. Despite occupying important positions, status, power, and authority in the eye of the people, women remain effaced in this grand action plan of WB. Instead it promotes an authoritative hold on knowledge of nature and its uses, which is the face of a public patriarchy that is still to come in a large way in north-east India.

But despite the enormous impact of conflict on women, they do not play a decisive role in conflict resolution and post-conflict reconstruction. As mentioned earlier, women are either perceived as victims or as healers, but never taken as decision-makers in the process. While full attention must be given to the survivors of armed conflicts, the method of reconstruction and rehabilitation must necessarily be within the empowerment and equality framework. Women perceive peace as a condition that is free of violence of any kind in society, and this implies the co-existence of all people with basic human dignity. The extremely low participation of women in decision making bodies—whether it be the traditional bodies or the modern democratic institutions like legislative assemblies—has also largely contributed to the impasse in the conflict resolution process.

References

Leys, Colin. 1996. *The Rise and Fall of Development Theory*, Indiana: University Press.

Kapoor, I. 2004. 'Hyper-self-reflexive development? Spivak on Representing the Third World 'Other". *Third World Quarterly*, 4(25): 627–47.

Spivak, G. 1999. *A Critique of Postcolonial Reason: Toward a Critique of the Vanishing Present*. Cambridge, MA: Harvard University Press.

Conflict, Democratic Rights, and Peace in Nagaland

Lanusashi Longkumer

The Background

In the contemporary world system premise defining the condition of democratic rights vary from culture to culture and from situation to situation which often eludes the core essence of human values and dignity that is enshrined in the Universal Declaration of Human Rights (UDHR) which asserts that 'all human beings are born free and equal in dignity and rights'. In many parts of the world the very essence of human freedom, value and dignity are undermined in social processes often rooted in the colonial past. Today, the scars of the colonial legacy can be observed in several regions over the question of nation building and identity based on 'national consciousness' that often lead to vicious cycles of repression under the neo-colonial polity. The conflicts and the question of democratic rights in Nagaland represent a classic example of the remnants of the colonial past, albeit with more complexities.

The formal end of the colonial rule had greatly influenced the geopolitical dynamics of the corridor between the Indian sub-continent and South-East Asia. Emergence of new States were marked by the subtle neo-colonialism launched through the creation of new States whereby many smaller nationalities were subjugated by stronger and more dominant nations. The Nagas, who were once a self-reliant sovereign republic occupying a vast tract of land wedged between the strategic tri-junction of China, Myanmar, and India, were denied the assertion of the geostrategic importance of their territory from the global perspective, while conversely, the expansionists viewed the region as 'frontier region' and was often targeted from the lens of 'Lebensraum' or living space. Circumstantially, the geostrategic position of Naga hills proved significant during the Second World War when the powerful Nippon Imperial army was halted by the British Allied troops in the great battle of Kohima (1944–45), putting an end to the war in this corner of Asian continent. This situation provided ample scope for squabbling over the region leading to successive waves of occupation of the Naga territory and different political settings in the post-colonial arrangements. Such geopolitical dynamics has resulted in a series of conflict situations and human rights concerns in Nagaland for the past more than six decades.

It is widely accepted that most theories and discourses on conflicts presently revolve around the question of community rights and social justice and the inability of the State to address the welfare of the people. However, considering the Indo–Naga conflict in its proper perspective it is imperative to recall the first Naga confrontation with the British expedition led by Captains Jenkins and Pemberton in 1832 intruding into the Naga territory in their search for a link route between Manipur and Assam. After many years of resistance and confrontation, the British colonial power created Naga Hills District in 1866. Subsequently the British tried both war and diplomacy while dealing with the Nagas. Although large parts of the Naga territory were controlled by the British, the local self-governance of the Naga village administrative system enjoyed almost complete autonomy. In a way, active administration was never enforced due to the policy of non-interference of the British government. The British showed no inclination or intention of controlling the eastern sector of the Naga territory, in the North East Frontier Agency (NEFA) and beyond. As a matter of fact, whatever was the understanding and truce arrived at between the Nagas and the British were respected and honoured. When the Simon Commission came to Kohima in 1929, the Naga representatives submitted a memorandum clearly stating that they should be left alone and independent just as the British found them. In recognition of the claim made by the Nagas to be treated separately from the rest of India, the Government of India Act, 1935 renamed the Naga Hills District as the 'Naga Hills Excluded Area' which was not subject to the jurisdiction of provincial acts or federal legislature but to be directly administered by the Governor. Furthering their stance, post-Independence, the Nagas rejected the Sixth Schedule of the Indian Constitution.

Neo-colonialism, Alienation and Conflict

The futility to convince Indian leaders compelled the Naga leaders to declare 'Naga Independence' on 14 August 1947.

The Nagas refused to merge with the nascent Indian nation on the grounds that they differed culturally, ethnically, and racially from it, nor did they share any historical memories or general sense of belonging with the Indians. The government of India was, however, implacably committed to the view that Nagaland was an integral part of India and subsequently imprisoned A.Z. Phizo, the then president of Naga National Council (NNC) and other leaders. In spite of these and other moves, the Nagas continued their dialogue with the Government of India (GoI).

To reaffirm their stance a referendum and plebiscite were conducted on 16 May 1951. In these, not a single Naga opted to be with India or Myanmar but to remain as free as before. This was followed by the total boycott of the first General Elections of India and the subsequent mass civil disobedience movement in Naga areas, which was crushed using extreme measures by the Indian administration. This was followed by requisition of able-bodied Nagas as porters with stiff sentences being served on villages for defiance of the order.

A delegation of Naga leaders had been assured by Mahatma Gandhi on 19 July 1947 that they would not be forced into joining India. But that was not to be. The then Prime Minister Jawaharlal Nehru was angered at a small ethnic group of seemingly illiterate tribesmen challenging the very concept of the newly born Indian nation. Evidently, in his letter to Medhi, the then Chief Minister of Assam, on the fate of the Nagas, Nehru wrote, 'under our constitution we split them up in different political areas; whether it is possible or desirable to bring them together again is for us to consider'. Under the new political design, Nagas were split up to join two separate countries of India and Burma (present Myanmar), further bifurcated by state political boundaries into four states within the Indian constitutional framework. The divide and rule policy of the British has been applied more discordantly. It not only divided the Naga polity but also the Naga society. Hence, in contravention to many universal values and norms and against many established concepts of academic domain today, Nagas found themselves in two world geographic regions of South and South-East Asia.[1]

Conflict, Militarisation, and Democratic Rights

With the departure of the British from the Naga Hills, the existing laws were fast replaced by new legislations, Acts, and laws which were imposed upon the Naga people. The nascent Indian government stepped up its show of military might with swift promulgation of the Assam Maintenance of Public Order (Autonomous District) Act, subsequently the Assam Disturbed Area Act, 1955 to enable the Assam Armed Police and Assam Rifles to carry out their armed operations unabated without any legal restraints. The militarisation process have roused many acts and legislations that were used to suit the colonial stakes which were used more rigorously in Nagaland and elsewhere in the 'disturbed areas' of the country.

The militarisation process of the state got markedly intensified following the en masse walk out by the Nagas from a public meeting jointly addressed by Nehru and the prime minister of Myanmar (then Burma), in Kohima on 30 March 1953. The Indian government responded with wrath by unleashing terror and intensified the military campaign of coercion and violence against the Nagas in order to make them submit to the Union of India. In 1954, the Indian Air Force 29th Squadron began aerial bombardment in Naga areas. NNC took the path of armed insurrection in 1954 when their attempts to open a dialogue to discuss the future of the Nagas were rejected.

From the very beginning in its attempt to contain the Naga resistance movement, the Indian government adopted brutal force as the prime measure while economics and diplomacy played auxiliary roles. Of all the years, the decade between 1956 and 1966 is remembered by many Nagas as the 'dark decade' when the scale of military operation was at its peak with grouping of villages, concentration camps, unprecedented and inhuman treatments, mass rapes, murders, arson, looting, and so on being unleashed with impunity. There was nearly one security troop for every adult male Naga in the Naga Hills. Villagers were brought to a central village primarily to cut off civilian support to the insurgents. While in Malaya, the counter-insurgency approach (Wham) was used for protecting the civilians against the insurgents by grouping and sheltering them by the government forces, in Nagaland the Indian version of grouping was the most 'unforgettable hellish experience' as recalled by many elderly Nagas, many of whom were victims of the military terror tactics.

Michael Scott, a member of the Peace Committee constituted by Indian government, recounts the scenario in the Naga hills:

> Public opinion in India and the world has been kept in ignorance of the true state of affairs in Nagaland since the concerted army action of 1956–57 when villages throughout the land were subjugated to the reign of terror ... villages were evicted, then population chased into the jungle, churches were desecrated by obscene acts and burned.

Within a relatively short time 190 villages in the Sema region, 60 villages in the Chakesang region, and 49 villages in the Ao region were burned among others. In all, more than 645 villages were reduced to rubble along with their granaries. Jawaharlal Nehru, however, while addressing the Lok Sabha, stated, 'I can say with a measure of confidence that on the whole, our Indian army have functioned with discipline and credit to themselves and in accordance with their own high traditions'. After decades of military coercion and campaign to tame the defiant Nagas, the promulgation of Armed Forces (Special Powers) Act, 1958, amended in 1972, provided for the highest degree of militarisation in Nagaland and other parts of north-east India. The essence of AFSPA is that it gives ample scope for declaring an area as 'disturbed', even if the state does not require it. Nagaland, being a 'disturbed area' as perceived by the government, was virtually ruled by the Indian military for most of the time. By 1960, the number of security forces shot up to 200,000 in Nagaland against a population of 369,200. Intensification of militarisation and security control over the land became blatant all over Nagaland between 1960s and 1980s. Since then more co-ordinated and low intensity warfare in the form of counter-insurgency operative programme was launched in all Naga areas. As part of the counter-insurgency programme, regular patrolling along the national and state highways and in all the strategic locations was a common practice. To prevent roadside ambush by the insurgents, regular clearing of the jungle of considerable distance was made mandatory in many strategic places which the villagers had to do within their village without any compensation or labour charges whatsoever.

During the 1990s the security forces and military have changed their strategy to a decidedly higher and more sophisticated programme using various forms of alluring enticement slogans such as 'Friends of the Hill People', 'Operation Good Samaritan', 'Sati Laga Force' (Friendly Force), etc. through its Army Development Group (ADG) and Military Civil Action (MCA). Under these policies the security forces, under the pretext of building schools, public Halls, and parks, have been acquiring community lands in all strategic areas. In the post-ceasefire period (1997) a major developmental activity being carried out is the unprecedented infrastructural development in all military camps and occupied areas. Within the past few years the security forces have succeeded in establishing many more camps and check posts in the public residential areas creating a war-like environment and creating a fear psychosis in the minds of the people. However, violence was not the only means by which the Indian government dealt with the Nagas. They extended major concessions by creating a separate state called Nagaland in 1963 with extra constitutional provisions in the form of article 371 (A) of the Indian constitution.[2] However, the creation of Nagaland state by carving out a portion from the Naga territory has been viewed by the Nagas as a deliberate attempt to divide the land and the people. As a matter of fact, the policy of grant of statehood was a measure of 'realpolitik' having multi-dimensional ramification on the future of the Nagas. The immediate outcome of the statehood was not only the physical division but more seriously also the division between the Nagas into moderate and radical/nationalists besides dividing them politically and socially.

The Peace Initiatives

For many decades, Naga civil society bore the brunt of the conflict situation. Countless widows, orphans, and families torn apart as a consequence of the situation, have been played out over several years leaving a cynical and often disillusioned society in its wake. Concomitantly, members of Naga civil society organizations who voiced their concern at the spiralling cycle of violence over the years have been the target of the establishment and often from the insurgents. They have been looked upon by the Indian State as pro-insurgent or anti-government and on many occasions they became victims of the violence. However, with the commencement of the ceasefire between the Nagas and the Indian government, the Naga civil society got a democratic space to push their agenda of peace building in the Indo–Naga conflict. The 'Journey of Conscience' undertaken by the Naga civil society and students to Delhi in 2000 to engage in dialogue with Indian students, human and civil rights groups, academicians, etc., was well reciprocated culminating in their travelling into different Naga areas in March 2001. This initiative brought in a new dimension for the larger participation of the people in the process. The civil societies of India and the Nagas were convinced that ceasefire should not only hold but it should pave the way for dialogue and negotiations towards finding a peaceful solution. Concurrently the prominent mass-based Naga organisations and churches have been persistently working towards strengthening the peace process and to bring the conflict to a logical conclusion. In this regard, the Naga Hoho,[3] Naga Mothers' Association (NMA), United Naga Council (UNC), Naga People's Movement for Human Rights (NPMHR), Naga Students' Federation (NSF), and other concerned organisations have been meeting the Indian leaders for endorsing the 'peoples voice' and asking for support for the on-going political process.

At another level, the Forum for Naga Reconciliation (FNR) was able to persuade the warring Naga underground factions to come to a common understanding through the signing of the 'Covenant of Reconciliation' on 18 September 2010. Though the process of reconciliation is often a tight rope walk, coming as it is after more than three decades of bitter conflict, the process has been well initiated and could bring down intensity of the conflict to a large extent.

Even after 15 years of ceasefire and several rounds of talks between the Naga leaders and the Indian government, there seems to be ponderous problem with no definite solution in sight. The initial years of ceasefire period was dissipated with unresolved issues like ceasefire coverage, high-handedness of the security forces vis-a-vis extortion, and factional clashes among the insurgents. These severely impeded the negotiation process from moving forward. Further, the Indian government's method of adopting modern diplomacy of conflict resolution based on double dealings and delaying tactics have created an atmosphere of suspicion and disillusionment among the Naga leaders and the people in general. In spite of all these hitches and challenges Nagas have demonstrated their resolve to have a political settlement to end the protracted conflict with India. The present ceasefire, unlike the 1964 ceasefire and peace talks which ended in a 'truce without a political settlement', offers wide scope for resolving the Indo–Naga conflict with participation of all sections of the people. It has seen through five successive Prime Ministers—P.V. Narasimha Rao, H.D. Deve Gowda, I.K. Gujral, Atal Behari Vajpayee, and Man Mohan Singh—whose assurances have been 'peace and political settlement of the Naga problem on the basis of historical proprieties'.

The possibility of an end to the political turmoil has received a boost with the recent averment of the Joint Action Forum (JAF) consisting of elected representatives of the ruling Democratic Alliance of Nagaland (DAN) and the Opposition Congress of the state of Nagaland unanimously attesting their decision to the central leaders that 'Nagas want solution and not election'. They further expressed their willingness to step down to make ways for the Naga political settlement. Realising the futility of an armed conflict, the surge is on for a collective effort from all stakeholders to find a logical solution. The present opportunity can, therefore, be taken as a win-win situation by both the Nagas and the Indian State to create more democratic space for an optimal, acceptable, and honourable settlement. This would entail invariably removing all the 'black laws' such as the AFSPA and demilitarising the entire Naga region for a meaningful peace, dignity, and solution. Even after more than six decades of perpetual violation of human and democratic rights of the people and several breakdowns of agreements and accords, the Naga people yet chose dialogue in the quest of an honourable political settlement, a challenge which India cannot discount.

Notes

1. In geographic paradigm the concept of a 'region' deals with the spatial variation and distinctiveness, with an emphasis on the interaction between human and spatial element.
2. Art 371(A) is an extra-constitutional Act created supposedly to protect the customary laws, traditions, land, and resources of the Nagas. The said article reads: 'Notwithstanding anything in this constitution, no Act of Parliament in respect of (i) Religious or social practices of the Nagas, (ii) Naga customary law and procedure, (iii) Administration of civil and criminal justice involving decision according to Naga customary laws, and (iv) Ownership and transfer of land and its resources, shall apply to the state of Nagaland unless the Legislative Assembly of Nagaland by a resolution so decide'.
3. Naga Hoho is the apex traditional Naga organisation represented by Nagas from across the Naga territory.

Select Bibliography

Alemchiba Ao. A Brief Historical Account of Nagaland. Jorhat: Janambhomi Publishers, 1970.

Census of India 1961, Vol XXIII, Nagaland, Superintendent of Census Operations, Nagaland, p. 3.

Irulu, Kaka D. Nagaland and India: The Blood and the Tears (Kohima: 2000), p. 99.

Iyer, V.R. Krishna, Human Rights: A Judge's Miscellany. Delhi: B.R. Publishing Corporation.

Longkumer, Lanu. 'Dialogue on self-determination: Geopolitical considerations of the Indo–Naga Conflict', paper presented at Workshop on Civilians and Citizenship: Ethnographic and Political Economy Perspectives on Civil War in South Asia, Delhi School of Economics, Delhi University, 18–20 February 2010.

Longkumer, Lanu and Toshimenla Jamir, Nagaland Land Alienation: Dynamics of Colonialism, Security and Development. Delhi: Aakar Books, 2011, p. 26.

Means, Gordon P. and N. Ingun Means. 'Nagaland, the agony of ending guerilla war', *Pacific Affairs* 09 (1966–67): 290.

Mullik, B.N. My Years with Nehru. Delhi: Allied Publishers, 1971, pp. 313–14.

Naga Hoho, 'Nehru's letter to Medhi', 13 May 1956, in 'Naga Hoho letter to Secretary General, United Nations,' Hague, 2011.

Nibedon, Nirmal, North East India: The Ethnic Explotion. New Delhi: Lancers Publishers, 1981, p. 28.

———. The Night of the Guerillas. New Delhi: The Lancer Press, 1978.

Samaddar, Ranabir, 'Ceasefire in Nagaland, but what worth it is!' in *Naga Resistance and the Peace Process*, Dossier No. 8, p. 58.

Scott, Michael. *The Nagas: India's Problem or the World's? The Search for Peace.* London: W&J Mackay, 1966, p. 41.

Singh, Sanjay Kumar. 'Naga accords: An instance of domination through negotiation', in Naga Resistance and the Peace Process. New Delhi: Other Media Communications, 2001, p. 48.

About the Contributors

Sukalpa Bhattacharjee is Professor of English at North Eastern Hill University, Shillong. She has authored or co-edited four books on North-East.

Rajeev Bhattacharyya was the Managing Editor of *Seven Sisters Post*. He had also worked with reputed national dailies. He specialises in North-East insurgency and its connection with our neighbouring countries and South East Asia.

Vijayalakshmi Brara is Associate Professor at Centre for Manipur studies, Manipur University. She specialises on cultural, gender, and governance issues. She has authored a book on North-East.

Partha J. Das is a leading environmental activist and scholar based in Guwahati.

Samir Kumar Das is Vice-Chancellor of the University of North Bengal. A Professor of Political Science at the University of Calcutta (on lien) he specialises on ethnicity, security, migration, rights, justice, and democracy.

Harekrishna Deka was formerly Assam's Director-General of Police. He is an eminent scholar, literateur, and Sahitya Academy Award winner.

Sanjoy Hazarika is Director, Centre for North-East Policy Research Studies, Jamia Millia Islamia University, New Delhi.

Sunil Kaul has been working in rural areas on issues that determine the health of poor and tribal communities. He founded the Action Northeast Trust (Ant), an NGO based in Bodoland, Assam.

Lanusashi Longkumer is a distinguished scholar based in Kohima, Nagaland.

Patricia Mukhim is Editor, *Shillong Times*.

E.N. Rammohan was formerly Director-General, Border Security Force. He is a distinguished writer on insurgency and counter-terrorism.

Neeraj Vagholikar works with Kalpavriksh, a voluntary agency in Pune.

Index